PRINCIPLES OF PERSEVERANCE

PRINCIPLES OF PERSEVERANCE

Wes Daughenbaugh

CREATION
HOUSE
A STRANG COMPANY

PRINCIPLES OF PERSEVERANCE by Wes Daughenbaugh
Published by Creation House
A Strang Company
600 Rinehart Road
Lake Mary, Florida 32746
www.creationhouse.com

Unless otherwise noted, Scripture quotations are from the Holy Bible, New International Version. Copyright © 1973, 1978, 1984, International Bible Society. Used by permission.

Scripture quotations marked NKJV are from the New King James Version of the Bible. Copyright © 1979, 1980, 1982 by Thomas Nelson, Inc., publishers. Used by permission.

Scripture quotations marked NAS are from the New American Standard Bible. Copyright © 1960, 1962, 1963, 1968, 1971, 1972, 1973, 1975, 1977 by the Lockman Foundation. Used by permission. (www.Lockman.org)

Scripture quotations marked KJV are from the King James Version of the Bible.

Author photo courtesy of Bruce Berg Photography

Cover design by Terry Clifton

Library of Congress Control Number: 2007920194
International Standard Book Number: 978-1-59979-165-4

First Edition

07 08 09 10 11 — 9 8 7 6 5 4 3 2 1
Printed in the United States of America

DEDICATION

The truths in this book are vital for all Christians, regardless of their maturity level. I have written this book for the entire body of Christ. In writing it, however, I speak directly to men and women who are career ministers. I dedicate this book to pastors, missionaries, prophets, teachers, evangelists, administrators of churches and para-church ministries, and to their mates who co-labor with them.

I once prayed that Jesus would teach me to love Him the way He wanted to be loved. He said, "Love me like Mary who sat at my feet. Love me like John who leaned on my breast. Love me like the Good Samaritan. Love me like the woman who anointed my feet. Love me like Abraham who always obeyed me."

From this I knew I was to love God's Word, spend intimate time in prayer with Him, help the hurting and suffering as if they were Jesus, and to always obey Him. But I did not know how to apply His Word: "Love me like the woman who anointed my feet."

I asked what He meant. He said, "My pastors are the feet of the body of Christ. They carry the weight of responsibility and take the most abuse." Since then, I do whatever I can to encourage and refresh ministers of every kind. It is my hope that these words will wash and anoint the "feet" of the body of Christ—those who carry the weight of responsibility for His body.

My heart's desire is that these truths will help renew your strength when you feel physically, spiritually, mentally, or emotionally exhausted. May you never join the crowd who quit and just offer Jesus Christ an excuse. Rather, may you be among the overcomers who always find some way to renew their strength and complete their assignment from heaven. May you show love to Christ with great perseverance like Abraham, who always obeyed.

TABLE OF CONTENTS

Introduction

THE CYCLE OF SUCCESS

May the Lord direct your hearts into
God's love and Christ's perseverance.
—2 Thessalonians 3:5—

The principles in this book apply to every Christian. However, I wrote it with pastors in mind. The ministry is challenging, difficult, and sometimes downright impossible in our own strength. But if we quit living holy, if we no longer obey the Lordship of Jesus, we could join a large group of surprised preachers who will say, "'Lord, Lord, did we not prophesy in your name, and in your name drive out demons and perform many miracles?' Then I will tell them plainly, 'I never knew you. Away from me, you evildoers'" (Matt. 7:22–23).

The term *perseverance* should be defined as "love that keeps on obeying." It is the step in the cycle of success that comes just before victory and great achievement. Jesus promised to reveal Himself to and through those who truly keep on obeying Him. This is the promise of intimacy with Him—and intimacy with God is the ultimate in having significance and being successful, secure, and satisfied.

"Whoever has my commands and obeys them, he is the one who loves me. He who loves me will be loved by my Father, and I too will love him and show myself to him" (John 14:21).

He will reveal Himself to you if you persist in obedience.

"If anyone loves me, he will obey my teaching. My Father will love him, and we will come to him and make our home with him" (John 14:23). He is promising to reveal Himself *through* you if you persist in obedience.

Self help and psychology can never give us the power necessary to persist in obedience to Christ. That power comes only from God Himself. This power is given to people who depend on God. Each principle in this book is really just another way to depend upon the Lord.

Perseverance is a great word—but not the greatest word when it comes to being a great achiever. Once on a prayer walk I asked the Holy Spirit, "What is the key word in being a great achiever?" He spoke to me and said, *Dependency.* That was a shock to me. It sounded so weak. *Tough, brilliant, creative,* or *persistent* were words I supposed might be the key to great achievement. God's word to me, *dependency*, was a surprise. Then the Holy Spirit gave me a wonderful lesson explaining why dependence is an even greater word than perseverance. It is called the cycle of success.

True success and achievement all begin with depending on God. This is where true wisdom, faith, love, and power come from. There are worldly achievers who depend on self and seem to be real winners in this life. But the kind of success we are talking about is the kind that will stand the test of God's judgment and not be burned up. It is success as God defines it.

The next step in the cycle of success is to seek God. We must seek God until we hear God, which is step three. It is when we hear God that spectacular, supernatural faith comes, for "Faith comes by hearing, and hearing by the word (voice) of God" (Rom. 10:17, NKJV). After hearing from God, we have His direction and the revelation of His will, which creates real faith. That brings us to the fourth step in the cycle of success—obeying God.

Obeying God is often a long-term thing, a hard and sometimes almost impossible thing. That is why the fifth step in the cycle of success is perseverance. We must keep on obeying God until we come to the sixth step—victory and achievement. Then we move on to the seventh step, completing the cycle by returning the glory to God.

The bottom drops out of the success cycle unless we persist in obeying God. But if we do keep on obeying, not only do we come to victory and achievement, but our intimacy with God is increased, which is the ultimate reward.

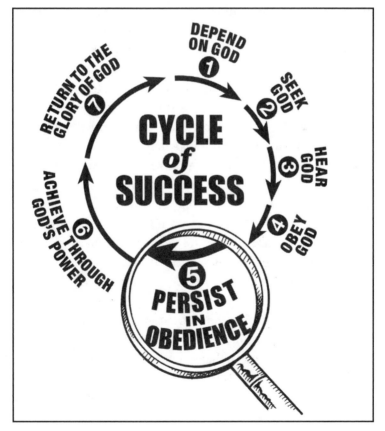

How many notes are in a musical scale? Most people think there are eight, but that is wrong. There are eight notes in an octave, but only seven in a musical scale: Do Ra Me Fa So La Te. Sing it, and it sounds incomplete. It only sounds right when you repeat the first note, thus starting a new musical cycle: Do Ra Me Fa So La Te Do.

In the same way, it is just not right to have only one cycle of success. After achievements and victories we must return the glory to God, completing the cycle and then immediately start a new one by going back to dependence. Real faith is always totally dependent on God, not self. God wants you to have one cycle of success after another, and He will give them to you if you actually do the steps. We get the power to persevere unto victory because we are depending on God. We have faith to persevere because we have sought God until we heard Him speak.

Whole books could be written about each step, particularly the step of seeking God or the step of hearing God. Many Christians and many churches have little spiritual power and few lasting achievements because they are not spending time earnestly seeking God, nor are they hearing from God. They are "religious," but they lack spiritual power. Expanding on those steps is beyond the scope of this book, but they are not difficult. Just do them—seek God, and keep seeking Him until you hear Him. If you do, you will be alive with faith, wisdom, love, direction, and spiritual power.

The subject of this book is the bottom of the cycle, perseverance; or in other words, "what to do instead of giving up." The apostles, the greatest of all achievers, the most victorious people with the most intimate relationships with Christ, persevered more than anyone else.

The things that mark an apostle—signs, wonders, and miracles—were done among you with great perseverance.

—2 CORINTHIANS 12:12

Great perseverance brings you to great success—if you are persevering in the will of God. Note what the apostle James says about perseverance. "Consider it pure joy, my brothers, whenever you face trials of many kinds, because you know that the testing of your faith develops perseverance. Perseverance must finish its work so that you may be mature and complete, not lacking anything" (James 1:2–4). Notice, too, that you will not lack any victory if you persevere in obedience to God. Continued obedience builds true Christlike character. This leads to Christlike victories of all kinds and eventual glorification with Christ. "Your attitude should be the same as that of Christ Jesus: who, being in very nature God, did not consider equality with God something to be grasped, but made himself nothing, taking the very nature of a servant, being made in human likeness. And being found in appearance as a man, he humbled himself and became obedient to death—even death on a cross. Therefore God exalted him to the highest place and gave him the name that is above every name" (Phil. 2:5–9).

It is important to know what perseverance is not. It is not a shot of spiritual Novocain to numb you so you can patiently let the devil beat you with blow after blow. No, it is more like getting into a tank and driving over the thorn hedges of the enemy until you reach your goal. Perseverance takes you somewhere—to victory, achievement, and intimacy with God. It takes you there regardless of the opposition.

The devil wants you to view perseverance as the mind-set of a ninety-eight-pound weakling who patiently lets a big bully kick sand in his face all day long. Satan does not want you to like perseverance, so he tries to spin it so that it appears weak instead of strong. Real perseverance—love that keeps on obeying—is incredibly strong. It is strong in God's power because its strength comes from depending on God in weakness. It develops mature Christlike character, and when we have Jesus' virtues we have Jesus-style victories.

The ability to persevere in obedience is vital for spiritual leadership. David is a great biblical example. Take the story of the burning of Ziklag in 1 Samuel 30. David had an army of six hundred men. They lived with the Philistines and had convinced the Philistine king that they were now loyal to him. David wanted to go to battle with them in the hopes of rescuing King Saul and other Israelite friends during the battle. But certain Philistine commanders rebuked their king for trusting a Hebrew and demanded that David be sent back to his town. When David and his troops arrived in Ziklag, they found that Amalekite raiders had kidnapped their families, stolen all their possessions, and burned their houses.

The battle-hardened men wept until they had no more strength to weep. Then they talked of stoning David. I imagine someone must have said, "If that blockhead David had killed King Saul when he had those two opportunities, none of this would have happened. Instead, he wanted to go to battle to rescue the guy who's trying to kill him. David is a nut and all this loss has happened to us because we're following an idiot. Let's kill him."

Things were looking bad when David started a new success cycle. Instead of quitting, he entered anew into dependence on God. He sought God earnestly. God spoke to him and assured him that if he pursued the enemy, he would overtake them and succeed in the rescue. David rallied his men for the pursuit because he had real faith that only comes from hearing God speak. He had heard the voice of God.

The next step was to obey and actually pursue. One-third

of his army could not cross the brook of Besor. I looked in a Hebrew dictionary to see what the word *Besor* meant because I had a hunch the meaning would be significant. It means "cheerfulness." Two hundred men were too exhausted to cross the little brook of cheerfulness. Your miracle is always on the other side of cheerfulness, by the way.

David continued the pursuit despite having to leave behind one-third of his small army. He kept obeying until he found an abandoned slave of an Amalekite raider. The man's cruel master had abandoned him three days earlier when he got sick. David revived him with water and food and the man promised to lead David and his men down to the enemy's camp.

There's a popular song that says, "I went to the enemy's camp and I took back what he stole from me." Christians sing that ignorantly. If you go to the enemy's camp without first depending on God, seeking God, and hearing God, you are likely to get killed. It is different when you have heard from God and go in true faith rather than presumption. The enemy's camp is not deserted. He is there—and he is armed and dangerous.

The Amalekites had spread over the land and were having a drunken party, reveling because of the plunder they had taken from their victims. David and his men had marched all day and began the battle at twilight. They fought the enemy all night long. Only four hundred enemy soldiers escaped. That means David's four hundred men had attacked a much larger army. They demonstrated the persistence that comes from depending on God. Remember, they were already tired when they arrived at Ziklag. Then they had become emotionally drained. They pursued the enemy all day long, and then fought in violent hand-to-hand combat all night long.

Persistence is not for the lazy or faint of heart. You are not exactly in a great comfort zone when you are persisting in obedience. Christ's persistence took him to the cross. David's persistence in battle took an all-out physical effort at a time when he must have longed to get some sleep.

This persistence in obedience brought David and his army to victory and success. You will never lack any victory if you persevere in obedience to God. Perseverance finishes its work and brings you to great achievement. David proved this. His enemies were routed, the captive families were recovered safely, and a huge amount of wealth was acquired.

David completed the cycle of success when he returned to the two hundred men he had left behind. Some troublemakers in his army insisted that these men not be allowed to share in the plunder. David's response shows that he gave all the glory to God for their victory:

> David replied, "No, my brothers, you must not do that with *what the* LORD *has given us. He has protected us and handed over to us the forces that came against us.* Who will listen to what you say? The share of the man who stayed with the supplies is to be the same as that of him who went down to the battle. All will share alike.
> —1 SAMUEL 30:23–24, EMPHASIS ADDED

Then David sent gifts to the elders of Judah from all the plunder. In the meantime, King Saul had been killed in the battle with the Philistines. The elders of Judah then decided to make David their king. Notice, God solves problems with problems and turns problems into blessings for those who truly walk in love. David's huge problem of a kidnapped family, burned house, and stolen property turned into his biggest miracle—the opening of the kingship to him.

Remember, God plays checkers with the devil. In checkers, the master player controls the game by purposefully moving a checker out where the enemy is forced to jump him. As that checker is removed from the board, he cries out, "Why did my master move me out and allowed me to get jumped? I do not understand." Meanwhile, our master is working his strategy to double jump the opponent and open up the king row. Soon, he speaks, "King me." The little checker is picked up and put on top of another checker, and becomes a king. As he is being put back into the game, as if with a new anointing and power, he says, "Ah—now I understand."

The longer I live, the more confident I have become that my Master will always be outsmarting the enemy even if He allows me to be removed from the board. I know it will only be a matter of time before I am back in the game with brand-new, God-given abilities and power.

In each chapter of this book, I am going to share with you a different tactic of perseverance—something to do, instead of giving up. Each tactic is accomplished by people who have depended on God, sought God, heard God, and have begun to obey God. Many times, the assignment from God is very difficult, or even impossible for the natural man to complete. The first steps may be done rather quickly, but the perseverance step, the bottom of the success cycle, may take a long time. It is in that very difficult time that we need these techniques of perseverance more than ever.

I have learned each of these twelve techniques of perseverance in the "school of the Spirit"—meaning, in fiery trials. They are like dear friends, tried and true. I introduce them to you with delight and great confidence, knowing that if you practice them you will achieve great victories.

Your ability to persist in obedience will be in direct proportion to how well you put each individual perseverance technique into practice. By reading this book, you will be able to spot areas where you are allowing your success to be drained away. You can troubleshoot your faith life, so to speak, and get it fixed up and running to victory.

Each individual perseverance technique can single-handedly cause you to win a certain victory. You may need a different technique for each different crisis. Each truth will add tremendously to your life. However, if you do them in concert—it will be like having your own army of mighty men. You can live in such a way as to be practicing all twelve at the same time. This is what the apostles did.

Please remember that the apostles are trainers and mentors for the rest of us. Paul wrote, "It was he who gave some to be apostles, some to be prophets, some to be evangelists, and some to be pastors and teachers, to prepare God's people for works of service, so that the body of Christ may be built up until we all reach unity in the faith and in the knowledge of the Son of God and become mature, attaining to the whole measure of the fullness of Christ" (Eph. 4:11–13).

As you observe these techniques of perseverance in the lives of the apostles, remember you are not just watching a movie for your own entertainment. You are watching a training film; you are supposed to imitate their way of life so that you become mature and Christlike in character. Then you will have Christlike victories, achievements, and Christlike intimacy with the Father.

Get ready to leave your excuses behind. I hope you will want to abandon them. They are quite useless. If you quit obeying God because the situation is impossibly difficult and suppose that will be an excuse God will accept—think again. God will not accept any excuse for ceasing to obey. He already knows it will be too hard for you in your own strength. But He is ready and willing to give you His strength so that when the task is complete, and the victory is sure, the glory will go to the One who so richly deserves it. He expects you to obey and persevere in obedience by learning how to depend upon Him.

Get ready to enter into a world where all things are possible. It is a world of the miraculous. It is the world of great achievers. It is the world of true spiritual leaders. It is the world of the Christlike, believing Christians who live to do the will of God and finish His work. It is the world of the totally committed. It is the world of the mature sons and daughters of God. It is a mountain so tall that the strong do not have the strength to climb it. Yet those who turned their weaknesses into dependence on God inhabit it. They are clothed in God's mighty power.

No one remains overwhelmed unless he or she chooses to lose. True overcomers cast away every excuse for remaining overwhelmed. They make choices that result in renewed power. The more you truly love God, the more likely you are to get overwhelmed in a real spiritual war. We are always closer to total dependence on God when we are overwhelmed. *You are supposed to get overwhelmed.* But when you do, you are not supposed to quit. You are not supposed to stay overwhelmed. Rather, you can learn apostolic techniques of dependence, each one capable of renewing your strength with God's supernatural power. We cannot wait vainly for the situation to change. We must act to change. We cannot just weakly hope the situation will someday, somehow, improve by itself. We must improve by God's grace.

We must reject the common choice to move backward into something we have the necessary strength to do. Rather than reduce the opposition to our level of strength, we must find God's strength to overcome the opposition.

Just as a speaker or author needs the anointing of God to teach, so the listener or reader needs the help of God to understand and apply the truths he or she is receiving. If you will read this book with a humble dependence upon the Holy Spirit, He will make these wonderful truths come alive to you and coach you in the daily application of them. Depend on God to help you digest these truths so completely that they will re-energize your spiritual reflexes. Then, the next time you are overwhelmed, you will be able to recover your strength much faster, complete that cycle of success, and begin a new one. If you practice these truths continually, what would easily overwhelm someone else will not overcome you. You may not even notice how really difficult the situations are because of the continual renewing of your spiritual power.

Before we get into the principles of perseverance, we need to realize that those who quit—who cease to obey and justify disobedience with excuses—are in great spiritual peril. Obedience is not optional with God. Jesus said, "To him who overcomes and does my will to the end, I will give authority over the nations" (Rev. 2:26). Jesus defines *overcoming* as doing the will of the Father until the end. Only those who persevere in obedience will inherit the Kingdom of God.

> He who overcomes will, like them, be dressed in white. I will never blot out his name from the book of life, but will acknowledge his name before my Father and his angels.
>
> —REVELATION 3:5

> Not everyone who says to me, "Lord, Lord," will enter the kingdom of heaven, but only he who does the will of my Father who is in heaven.
>
> —MATTHEW 7:21

> Because of the increase of wickedness, the love of most will grow cold, but he who stands firm to the end will be saved.
>
> —MATTHEW 24:12–13

The blood of Christ is a covering for our imperfect obedience. As long as we are attempting to be Christlike and our sincere desire is to please God, we will be viewed by God through the blood of Jesus and appear perfect and without fault, absolutely holy and free from accusation. (See Colossians 1:21–23.) If we move away from the hope held out in the gospel, we move out from under this blood covering and God would see and judge our sin.

The "hope held out in the gospel" is not the hope of heaven, but the hope of "Christ in you, the hope of glory" (Col: 1:27). Many hope to go to heaven, but have thrown away their hope of being Christlike in this earth. They do not want to be like Jesus. They have moved out from under the holy blood covering.

There are two ways believers can move out from under the holy blood covering of Christ—rebellion and idolatry. Rebellion refuses to obey or submit to God's authority. Idolatry puts something else ahead of God. The grace of God does not cover either one of these unless repentance has been sought of God.

If we die in rebellion or idolatry, the good things we did and the faith we had are forgotten completely by God so that He would say, "I never knew you." God will either forget our sin or our righteousness. When a person repents, it means they want to live differently. They are not merely sorry they got caught, they want to be Christlike in their lifestyle. Their sins will be forgotten. But Christians who think the holy blood of Jesus is a covering for willful sin—and who die unrepentant—will be shocked to find that God forgot their former righteousness:

> But if a righteous man turns from his righteousness and
> commits sin and does the same detestable things the
> wicked man does, will he live? None of the righteous
> things he has done will be remembered. Because of the

unfaithfulness he is guilty of and because of the sins he
has committed, he will die.

—EZEKIEL 18:24

As long as we are trying to serve God perfectly, He will
view our obedience as perfect in His sight. But the blood of
Jesus has never been, and never will be, a covering for rebellion or idolatry. "If we deliberately keep on sinning after we
have received the knowledge of the truth, no sacrifice for sins
is left, but only a fearful expectation of judgment and of raging
fire that will consume the enemies of God" (Heb. 10:26–27).

Therefore, the subject of persevering love is of extreme
importance for spiritual leaders and believers alike. By
persevering in obedience, we become great achievers. We
experience full intimacy with God. We will inherit all that
God has promised to the overcomers. We will escape the
judgment given to "wicked, lazy servants" (Matt. 25:26), who
quit obeying and only give God excuses instead of obedience.

"Once you were alienated from God and were enemies
in your minds because of your evil behavior. But now he has
reconciled you by Christ's physical body through death to
present you holy in his sight, without blemish and free from
accusation—if you continue in your faith, established and
firm, not moved from the hope held out in the gospel" (Col.
1:21–23). The hope held out in the gospel is stated further
down in this passage, "To them God has chosen to make
known among the Gentiles the glorious riches of this mystery,
which is Christ in you, the hope of glory" (Col. 1:27).

Salvation is not a free ticket to heaven. It is the right to
become a full-grown son of God. "But as many as received
him, to them gave he power to become the sons of God, *even*
to them that believe on his name" (John 1:12, KJV, emphasis
added). The word *sons* here means fully grown sons.

Imagine a man coming to the gate of heaven waving a

ticket. "Hey, God, let me in. I have my free ticket to heaven because I prayed the Sinners Prayer." God will say, *I did not give away any free tickets to heaven. That's a counterfeit. I gave out tickets that gave people the right to grow up in Christ in all things. What did you do with that ticket?*

The man says, "I did not want to be like Christ. I just wanted to get into heaven. So I threw away the original ticket you gave me and picked up this other one that says 'Free ticket to heaven.'" To that man God will say, *You are not getting in here.*

So many modern-day Christians act like obedience to God is completely optional. They have thrown away their true salvation—a ticket that gave them grace to be Christlike. In its place they have a substitute ticket that turns the grace of God into a license for immorality. But you, dear friend, can be an overcomer. You can keep your faith in Christ, and you can persevere in obedience. God's grace will give us power to obey. God's grace will even cover imperfect but sincere obedience making it appear perfect in God's sight. God's grace will always teach us how to respond in all of life's situations the way Jesus would. But God will never be mocked. We are saved by faith, and real faith bears the fruit of obedience. When it comes to obeying God, overcomers never quit.

Chapter 1

ADOPT THE HEART MOTIVE OF JESUS

*So whether you eat or drink or whatever you
do, do it all for the glory of God.*
—1 Corinthians 10:31—

There is a motive that moves mountains, and it is the very essence of heart purity. It is a transforming motive that works through your life like yeast working through dough, until it permeates everything you do, large or small. Anything done from this motive has eternal meaning. It is the master key that opens the door to answered prayer, anointed ministry, the revealed will of God, and Christlike courage. It is the master motivation of perseverance, the main thing that keeps you going when the going gets incredibly tough. *I'm speaking of the heart motive of Jesus, His burning desire to bring glory to His Father.*

This is the motivation that got me going in the ministry and created the momentum that has carried me through many great difficulties. If a train is already stopped, a tiny block of wood in front of a wheel can keep it stopped. But if the train has already built up momentum and is moving at high speed, not even a brick wall built across the track can stop it. Before you can build unstoppable momentum in your obedience to God, you will need this motivation to get you started.

The looming crucifixion experience was like a barricade to the obedience of Christ. Jesus knew he would be betrayed, denied, forsaken, falsely accused, rejected, denied justice, tortured, blasphemed, and murdered. Yet, despite that huge brick wall built across the track of his obedient love for the Father, Jesus was unstoppable. The momentum that had built up from his motive was going to propel Him, smashing through and carrying Him on to resurrection, vindication, and exaltation. It will do the same for you, but first it has to get in you and become your controlling motivation.

In my own life, many brick walls have been built across the track of my obedient love for my heavenly Father. I remember crashing through those barricades. I remember the noises and the blasts. But not once did I come to a stop and have to get re-motivated to get going again. That is why I want to spend time telling you how that motivation got me started rather than trying to describe how it keeps me going. I do not go looking for this motivation when things get hard. It is already inside me and it is in control. Its force, ferocity, and fire do not diminish when I pass through the swamp of despair, the fog of confusion, or a frontal attack by the devil.

For me, it all began with a revelation of the heart of Jesus. I was nineteen-years-old, in my second year of a three-year Bible college. I had been a born-again Christian for six years. I was reading the words of Jesus in John 17:

> Father, the time has come. Glorify your Son, that your Son may glorify you. For you granted him authority over all people that he might give eternal life to all those you have given him. Now this is eternal life: that they may know you, the only true God, and Jesus Christ, whom you have sent. I have brought you glory on earth by completing the work you gave me to do. And now, Father, glorify me in your presence with the glory I had with you before the world began.
>
> —JOHN 17:1-5

I said out loud, "He's asking for the glory. Isn't that wrong?" The Holy Spirit spoke to me, *Read it again.* Then God illumined this text so that I saw Christ's heart motive. It was as if Jesus was saying, "Father, I brought you glory down here by completely finishing the work you gave Me to do. Now I ask for a higher heavenly platform so that from there I might bring you even more glory. Glorify your son, (the request) that your son may glorify You, (the motive)."

Jesus was not into self-glorification. So much love for the Father filled the heart of Jesus that He had a burning desire to bring glory to the Father—by any means and no matter what the cost. After this initial revelation, God opened my eyes to see this heart motive of Jesus in other verses throughout the Gospel of John. Take time to meditate on these:

> How can you believe if you accept praise from one another, yet make no effort to obtain the praise that comes from the only God?
>
> —JOHN 5:44

> He who speaks on his own does so to gain honor for himself, but he who works for the honor of the one who sent him is a man of truth; there is nothing false about him.
>
> —JOHN 7:18

> I am not seeking glory for myself; but there is one who seeks it, and he is the judge.
>
> —JOHN 8:50

> And I will do whatever you ask in my name, so that the Son may bring glory to the Father.
>
> —JOHN 14:13

For the next year God sifted my motivation. I was a soloist for the Zamar Chorale, the college choir of Eugene Bible College. Before one performance God asked me, *Why do you want to sing tonight?* I answered, "Well, I want everyone to see that I am a good singer." Immediately I was convicted, and I said, "No, I want to sing so that everyone will see You." Then an anointing from God bonded with me. People were blessed when I sang, and the director chose to let me sing again at the next concert.

I was once preparing to sing a song I had written. The Holy Spirit asked me, *Why do you want to sing that song you wrote instead of one from the hymnal?* Looking into my heart, I answered honestly, "I want everyone to see that I am creative, poetic, and talented, as well as a good singer." There it was again—the self-glorifying motive of Satan. When I saw its ugliness, I changed and said, "Father, I want to sing this song because it has a special message that reveals you. I want to get this truth across." Almost immediately, the Holy Spirit anointed me again.

God questioned my motives for a long time until Christ's pure motive was thoroughly in control; "rooted" in me, so to speak. When graduation was at hand, we had a Senior Day during which the seniors of the class described what they would be doing after graduation. One said, "I have been voted in to be a pastor." One said, "I have been hired to be a youth director." Another said, "I have been given the responsibility of directing a choir." My turn came. I said, "I do not know *where* I am going or *what* I am going to do. I only know the *why*. Whatever I do, I will do it to bring glory to God." When that service concluded, I wept at the altar as I expressed my heart's desire to be used to bring glory to God.

Upon graduation, I found employment in a veneer mill, with physical ten-hour days, five-days-per-week. All day long I would think about how I could bring glory to God. One night, after an exhausting day at work, I knelt in our living room and prayed, "Oh, Father, if all You'd let me do is shine some pastor's shoes, I would be so grateful. But please, let me have some way of bringing you glory."

Soon I received a call from a local pastor who had been tipped off by my mother-in-law, Wilma Wilson. We lived in a mobile home in Goshen, Oregon. I had been skipping around to any church that would let me sing an occasional song. Pastor Cliff Traub called, interviewed my wife and I, and asked me to become his choir director. Bonnie became the church pianist.

Although I did not read music, I jumped at this opportunity. I was happy to have some way to bring glory to God. After about two weeks of that, my spirit felt uneasy. If you left your socks on when you took a shower something would not feel right. That was the way my spirit-man felt. I prayed, "God, do you want me to study the piano and learn how to read music so I can be a great choir director? What's my main ministry supposed to be here?" God spoke to me, *Your primary ministry here is to be a soul winner.*

I was excited. In another prayer meeting I asked, "How many souls can I believe you for?" God spoke again, *As many as the stars of the heavens.* Now I was really excited. I immediately went street witnessing, but I had a rough first night. I prayed, "God, how can I win as many as the stars of the heavens when I am having trouble winning even one?" God spoke again, *Start with children. They are the good ground of Matthew 13.*

You see, the motivation to bring God glory was acting as the "usher of God." It had led me to the cross where I repented and turned from the motivation of Satan—self-glorification. Now it was ushering me to the mountaintop from where I could view a great vision.

I became a bus captain for the church and excelled to the point where I was promoted to directing the entire bus ministry. The church hired me part-time, then after six months I became a full-time minister.

In Western Oregon we get a lot of rain, and Saturday bus visitation was often a soggy affair. It took about five hours on Saturday to effectively visit my bus route. Sometimes my flesh wanted to watch sports on TV and I would confess,

"I do not feel like doing my bus route today. What do you feel like, Lord?" He always felt like it. So I would pray, "Let me feel what you feel." Then I would go do the route.

Eventually we had more than one thousand children signed up and my staff visited them each week. We brought in more than five hundred each Sunday for the last three years I was on staff. The anointing just kept on increasing in my life because the "usher of God," the heart motive of Jesus, was also taking me to the "spout where the glory comes out."

Years later, I was pastoring a church in Omaha, Nebraska. One Wednesday night, I was beginning a series on the gifts of the Holy Spirit. I spent the entire service teaching about the heart motivations of Jesus. I taught on three of Christ's motivations—His desire to bring glory to the Father, His seeking, searching love for people, and His hatred of evil:

> For the Son of Man came to seek and to save what was lost.
>
> —LUKE 19:10

> The reason the Son of God appeared was to destroy the devil's work.
>
> —1 JOHN 3:8

After teaching about these three motivations and majoring on Christ's desire to bring glory to the Father, I told the people I would like to pray for them to be filled with these motivations. People came forward and stood across the front of the sanctuary. I began to lay hands on them and pray. One man in the church, an air force colonel, was often used in the gift of discerning of spirits. God would open his eyes and he would see what things looked like in the spiritual realm. As I prayed for the people, he saw in a vision what was happening. Each person I prayed for was being covered in a white spiritual liquid.

He asked God, "Father, what's that white stuff you are putting on the people that looks like Elmer's Glue?" God spoke to him, *That's the motivation of Jesus. When I send my angels with spiritual gifts, those gifts will stick to that motivation. But if that motivation dries up the gifts will fall off.*

That was a profound revelation. Even a child can understand that concept. It explains why so many churches that believe in the gifts of the Spirit have so few manifestations of them. It explains why so many ministers lose the anointing and quit the ministry. We all need to determine that this will not happen to us, but rather that we will always be spiritually sticky with the motivations of Christ, especially His desire to bring glory to the Father.

Since that first revelation about the heart of Jesus and His passionate desire to bring glory to the Father, I have prayed daily that the Holy Spirit would use me to bring glory to God. I think about it all day long—every day—even after all these years. I have come to the point where I am conscious of what I say and think. When negative emotions are building, I am conscious of it and resist them. I am always looking for some little way to bring God glory. It is not a motive I turn on in church services. It is in my heart when I go to the post office and open the door for a lady with a child and let her get in line in front of me.

When I stay in a motel, I always turn out all the lights in the room if I go for a walk. Motel rooms do not have one master switch. They have about eight different lamps. I turn them all out to save money for the motel owner. When I stay in private homes, I wipe down the shower with a towel to keep soap scum from building up—just like my wife trained me to do at home. I do this because Jesus said, "Do to others as you would have them do to you" (Luke 6:31). I want to please Him constantly, and I know that none of this goes unnoticed by Him.

Each day I pray God will help me rightly divide my time in the different priority areas of life. In my thirty-four years of full-time ministry I have made great mistakes and sinned ignorantly even while I was trying with all my heart to glorify God. I worked an average of eighty-seven hours per week during the first seven years of my ministry. I was completely unaware of the emotional needs of my wife. So I thank God for the holy covering blood of Jesus. As God views me through that blood, He sees me holy in His sight and I am free from the accusations of Satan. (See Colossians 1:21–22.) I know I do not glorify God perfectly—but it is my constant objective. I am not discouraged when I find out that some effort of obedience was misguided. I repent, of course. I am trusting in the blood of Christ, not my own good works. I do not try to fill my day with little deeds of kindness to earn God's love for me. I do that to show my love for Him, and when I find some better way of doing it, I change.

There is a strong connection between pleasing God and having a strong anointing of the Holy Spirit. Jesus said, "The one who sent me is with me; he has not left me alone, for I always do what pleases him" (John 8:29). When we crave to bring God glory we always think about how to please Him. Then, an abiding anointing will be in us and upon us because we have so much in common with the Holy Spirit. The Holy Spirit wants to bring glory to Jesus, who said, "He will bring glory to me by taking from what is mine and making it known to you" (John 16:14).

Each Member of the Trinity wants to bring glory to the other two Members. The Son seeks to glorify the Father. The Father seeks to glorify the Son. Jesus said, "I am not seeking glory for myself; but there is one who seeks it, and he is the judge" (John 8:50). In the Book of Revelation, when the resurrected Christ speaks, He says, "Hear what the Spirit says to the churches" (Rev. 3:22). By doing that, Jesus was bringing glory to the Holy Spirit. The Father glorifies the Son. The Son glorifies the Father. The Spirit glorifies the Son. The Son glorifies the Spirit. The Father, Son, and Holy Spirit are perfectly united so that they are one God.

Here is how this practically applies to you. Suppose you want to bring glory to Jesus. The Father and the Holy Spirit are both going to be very interested in you—because that is what they want to do. I know that if I want to bring glory to the Father both Jesus and the Holy Spirit are going to be very interested in me—because that is what they want to do. We are going to get along well all day long in every situation because we are on the same wavelength, so to speak. We are moving in the same direction, toward the same goal.

When you crave to bring glory to God, the Holy Spirit will show you how to do it and empower you to do it. The devil cannot stop you from bringing glory to God when you want to, because the infinite power of the Holy Spirit is going to help you. The devil has to try to disrupt your motivation first to get you distracted. Jesus put it this way, "Still others, like seed sown among thorns, hear the word; but the worries of this life, the deceitfulness of wealth and the desires for other things come in and choke the word, making it unfruitful" (Mark 4:18–19).

When people are not motivated to bring God glory, spiritual weeds can grow all around them. They are worried rather than on fire with love for God. Instead of yearning to bring God glory, they only think about getting rich. They desire other things so that their focus is not upon pleasing God.

I want to be wise so I can bring glory to God, therefore I learn about money management and investment strategies. I want to be a good steward and please God with my attitude toward money. My desire to bring glory to God keeps me

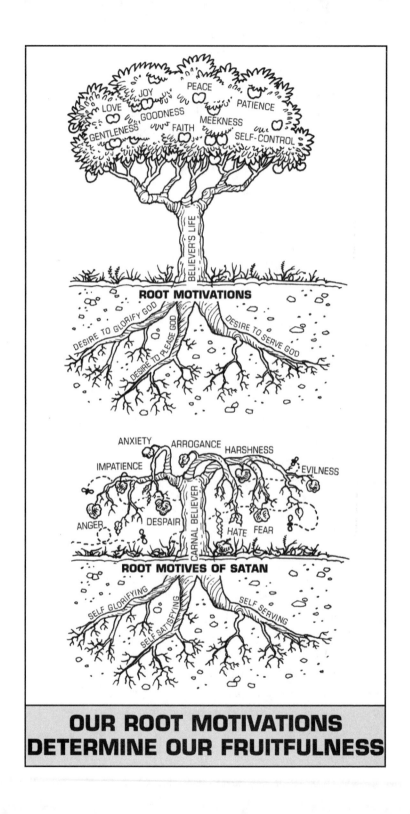

OUR ROOT MOTIVATIONS
DETERMINE OUR FRUITFULNESS

spiritually safe. I can prosper without being corrupted. Consider this: a burning passion to bring glory to God will not only keep you empowered and anointed—it will also keep you from straying into sin. That is why this motive is the very essence of heart purity.

As Christ approached the cross, He had to persist in obedience. What kept Him going? He just went back to His root motivation. What got Him going, kept Him going. Jesus prayed, "'Now my heart is troubled, and what shall I say? "Father, save me from this hour"? No, it was for this very reason I came to this hour. Father, glorify your name!' Then a voice came from heaven, 'I have glorified it, and will glorify it again'" (John 12:27–28).

If this motive gets you going, it will always keep you going. It is the most important of these twelve principles of perseverance. You simply cannot complete a true cycle of success without this motivation. No one can persist in Christlike obedience with a Satanic root motivation of self-glorification. So, what is in your heart? Does Christ's golden motive possess you? Ask the Holy Spirit to show you the truth about your heart motivation. Then adjust it, with His help, so that what motivates Jesus Christ also motivates you.

Sins of all different kinds trip up ministers and bring them to ruin. As a young ministerial student, I was warned to avoid coveting "the gold, the girl, and the glory." That meant that bad spiritual fruit comes from bad root motivations such as greed, lust, and pride. However, no one warned me that bitterness and self-pity would be even greater temptations. *We avoid sin when our desire to glorify God is our strongest desire.*

Purity of heart motivation determines purity in every other area of life. If you would steal the glory from God, your heart would not be troubled if you stole your neighbor's wife or your boss's money. When our motivation is pure, the desire to please and glorify God keeps us safer than any other technique, accountability network, or spiritual discipline. And, if our motivations are not pure? Temptations will readily jump over whatever boundaries we have set up and bond to us. The overcomers Jesus Christ speaks of in the Book of Revelation will all have exactly the same motivation—Christ's own passionate desire to glorify the Father.

Chapter 2
Decide to Pray Through

Then Jesus told his disciples a parable
to show them that they should
always pray and not give up.
—Luke 18:1—

The first apostles had to learn that prayer and giving up are exact opposites. You have given up when you have quit praying. "Praying through" is more than just prayer, however. It is a prevailing kind of prayer, more violent and desperate than mere "prayer." It is the kind of prayer where we pray until God hears us or we hear from God. It may involve fasting. In this kind of prayer, one lays hold of God just as Jacob wrestled with the angel and said, "I will not let you go unless you bless me" (Gen. 32:26). Jacob had wrestled with this "man" from heaven all night long. Then the angel touched Jacob's hip and it was wrenched in its socket. Still Jacob would not let go, though he was wounded. It was obvious to Jacob that the angel could just touch him in the head or heart and kill him.

Still, Jacob held on and would not let go. His need was desperate. His brother Esau was coming to meet him with an army of four hundred men. You do not bring an army to a family reunion unless you are bent on evil. Esau had vowed to kill Jacob and had stewed in the juices of hatred for twenty years. Jacob needed a miracle. If he died wrestling with that angel, it was all the same—his brother was going to kill him anyway. That was why he prayed with abandon—with an all-out effort to get God to hear his cry to be blessed.

The messenger from heaven blessed him with a new name, Israel. Jacob had prayed to be saved from his brother before the angel had come. God had already given him a strategy to send flocks of different animals ahead of him to appease his brother's anger. But when the angel blessed him, a gift of faith came to Jacob through God's voice. He knew he had the answer. He knew he would be delivered from Esau's wrath. He had prayed through. He already had the victory as he approached his brother and bowed down seven times to show his sincerity and humility. The estranged brothers had a great loving reunion and no blood was shed. (See Genesis 33.)

Jacob had been commanded by God to return to Canaan. But, in order to keep obeying God when he heard the news of his brother coming with four hundred armed men, Jacob had to use a principle of persevering love. He had to either pray through, or quit obeying and run for his life.

In January 1997, I began traveling as a teacher/evangelist from a base in Omaha, Nebraska. As summer approached, I only had one scheduled meeting for July and it was in Illinois. Nothing was scheduled for August. It was nearly June when that only meeting for July called and cancelled. Traveling ministers need lead time to book meetings in churches. Six to eighteen months is the norm. Booking anything with less than three months lead time is nearly impossible. I was in a bad situation.

The devil reminded me that I was already out of time. A voice seemed to be saying, "You've got to quit the ministry and go get a job selling used cars or insurance. It is already too late. It is over. You have to quit the ministry." Well, I had to quit or do something. I chose to pray all night long. It was that desperate kind of prayer that I call "praying through."

I did not really know what to ask for or what to ask God to do. The answer to my dilemma was a mystery to me. I prayed about six hours in tongues; that is, I prayed "in the Spirit." This kind of prayer was common in the first-century church. The apostle Paul said, "I thank God that I speak in tongues more than all of you" (1 Cor. 14:18). He also wrote, "Anyone who speaks in a tongue does not speak to men but to God. Indeed, no one understands him; he utters mysteries with his spirit" (1 Cor. 14:2).

When the next morning arrived, I knew what to do. I believe the Holy Spirit had helped me pray the mysterious answer and then gave me an interpretation to my prayer. I knew that the meeting in Illinois (east of Omaha) had cancelled because I was supposed to go west. I also knew that I was to take my wife and two daughters, along with our dog and cat, to Oregon. They were to stay with my wife's parents while I held meetings in the Pacific Northwest. Then, in between the meetings, I could vacation with my family.

That morning, I began calling pastors in Oregon and Washington. I told them, "I am coming out there this summer to vacation with my family and if you book a meeting there'll be no transportation costs." I booked five meetings in one morning. Five meetings booked in one morning would be a great answer to prayer even with lots of lead time. With only a month lead time, this was clearly a miracle.

We took two cars to Oregon. My wife, two daughters, our dog and cat—we all moved in with Bonnie's parents in their small three bedroom, one bathroom house in Oakridge, a small mountain town. A local realtor came by. He said,

"Look, the house next door is for sale. It is vacant, and I am the listing agent. I am going to let you use that house so you will have an extra bathroom and you can set up your office in one of the bedrooms. In fact, you can move in furniture if you want and live there. I will ask your permission before showing the house." He gave me the key. We used its extra bathroom and I had plenty of room for my office during the entire month of July. You see, by praying in tongues with the help of the Holy Spirit, I had prayed in the mind and will of God. My natural mind could not have known to even ask for a vacant house next door.

When I pioneered a church in Omaha, we began meeting in the Holiday Inn. The church was not paying me a salary. I was getting five hundred dollars a month in salary from the Nebraska District of the Assemblies of God, and another two hundred fifty dollars each month from my brother-in-law's church, Creswell Christian Center. But I needed a children's pastor who could do children's church while I was doing adult church. That way, with something excellent for kids, we could grow much faster.

I went into a cornfield and prayed in tongues for two hours. How to get a children's pastor was a mystery to me. I prayed in the Spirit so that the Holy Spirit could help me pray through to the mysterious answer. At the end of two hours, I knew what to do. Again, I believe God gave me the interpretation to what I had already prayed. Paul wrote, "For this reason anyone who speaks in a tongue should pray that he may interpret what he says" (1 Cor. 14:13). Most of the time when I pray in tongues, I do not get an interpretation; I have an increased sense of peace.

I knew that I should call Pastor Ken Brown in Arnold, Missouri. He had a small Bible college in his church. I knew that there would be a student who had just graduated and that this student would come and work for free as my children's pastor. Still, I thought it odd that anyone would graduate students in August. I prayed, "Lord, how can that be? No one graduates students in August." God spoke by silence. When He is silent, it is often because He has already told you what to do.

I called Pastor Ken Brown. He said, "Yes, we graduate in August and all our students have already left for ministry assignments except for one young man. He does not know where he's supposed to go, so he's waiting on God until God shows him what to do."

I asked, "What's his major?" Pastor Brown answered, "Child evangelism."

Immediately I drove the five hundred miles to Arnold, Missouri, and interviewed the young man. I told him I only had a great opportunity to win souls and that the city was one of the greatest in America. He came and worked for free for the next ten months. Then, just before I was able to start paying him a salary, he had a moral failure and had to leave. But I will always remember what a huge blessing he was and how much he helped me get the church going. After he left, we were able to hire a children's pastor.

This is a great truth: "It does not cost anything to pray." So many church leaders say, "We cannot afford to hire staff. We cannot afford a new building." But all things are possible to those who believe God. When we pray with the help of the Holy Spirit He will search the mind and will of God and help us pray according to God's will. John wrote, "This is the confidence we have in approaching God: that if we ask anything according to his will, he hears us. And if we know that he hears us—whatever we ask—we know that we have what we asked of him" (1 John 5:14–15).

You may have been taught that not all Christians will speak in tongues. Not all Christians are used by the Holy

Spirit to "prophecy" in tongues. That is when the flow comes down from heaven and out to the people—when God is speaking to the people through tongues and interpretation. That is a special gift of the Spirit. But every Christian needs to be able to pray in the Spirit, where they speak to God in a language their minds do not understand. That is praying with the aid of the Holy Spirit. In this way, they can pray through to the mysterious answers about which their natural minds would have no knowledge. It is absolutely God's will to fill you with the Holy Spirit and enable you to enjoy this wonderful kind of prayer.

To say you do not need it would be foolish. No human mind, no matter how brilliant, can know all the mysterious answers to big problems. But God knows and can help us pray through to these miraculous results. What is sad is that so many Christians who have received the baptism of the Holy Spirit do not pray much in the Holy Spirit.

Your ability to persist in obedience is directly related to your ability to pray through. It is possible to pray through using your natural mind. Those who pray with all their heart and yet do not speak in tongues can achieve wonderful breakthroughs in prayer as well. It is just a whole lot easier when you can pray in tongues. Praying five hours that way is so much easier than trying to figure out what to say with your natural mind.

Remember, the apostle Paul wrote, "The things that mark an apostle—signs, wonders, and miracles—were done among you with great perseverance" (2 Cor. 12:12). He is the same guy who wrote, "I thank God that I speak in tongues more than all of you" (1 Cor. 14:18). Your perseverance is in direct proportion to your amount of prevailing prayer.

To the vast majority of Christians I could truthfully say, "I thank my God I pray in tongues more than all of you." It is a usual thing for me to pray from one to three hours a day in tongues. I usually do this in the early morning when I wake up. I may lie in bed or just go lay on a couch and pray quietly that way. I may pray that way on a prayer walk. It is easy, very relaxing, and I am able to really cast my cares on God that way. It is spiritually edifying to adore God in that language of love. Then, having prayed through the day already, I get up and fight my battles in the arena of God's peace. I do not pray so much because I am so spiritual. Usually, I pray that much because I am in a mess and I am desperately in need of God's help. Many times, however, I pray in the spirit just as a way to adore God and give Him empowered worship. It brings great peace to our souls when we spend time just worshiping God with true adoration.

Here's a great truth: when we fight Satan in the arena of God's peace, we always win. Satan has to get us out of the arena of peace in order to prevail over us. That is why he cannot defeat a church that stays in unity. First, he has to get the church out of peace and into strife. He always wins the battle when he fights a Christian on his own turf—outside the arena of God's peace.

The Bible says, "The God of peace will soon crush Satan under your feet" (Rom. 16:20). The Lord showed me a great truth based on this verse. God wants us to get into His peace first, before we try to crush Satan. We do that by praying through. Then, having already attained God's peace, we fight our battle with Satan in the arena of God's peace. We *always* win in that arena.

The man or woman who prays a lot in the Spirit, early in the morning, is going to begin their day in the arena of God's peace. They'll be able to defeat the devil's attacks and strategies. But the believer who thinks, "I will have to defeat these problems before I can have peace," is living in deception.

It is a great lie, a great satanic deception to believe that you will have to win your battle first, in order to have peace. Most Christians are living in that common but deadly deception.

This is why we should have regular prayer fellowship with God each morning. Whether you pray in your natural language or pray in the Spirit, when you seek God you are entering into the second step of the cycle of success. By praying through you move to the third step in the cycle—you hear from God and God hears you. When God hears you, He gives you an assurance of peace in your heart, so that, in effect, you have heard from Him as well. Then you are able to move on to the fourth step of the cycle of success—obeying God.

In the case of the children's pastor, or the time I booked five meetings in one day on the West Coast—my obedience was predicated on having already completed steps two and three of the cycle of success. I had prayed through.

When we do not begin our day with prayer we are at a disadvantage. We haven't prayed through the problems we face to the mysterious answers we need. We haven't really gotten into the arena of God's peace. So if you'd like to have great achievements, great victories, and great intimacy with God— the rewards that come from persevering in obedience—then you must develop the habit of praying through. Please do not wait for a crisis like Jacob had to pray through. Pray through before you come to the crises. That's the best way. And if you do run into great trouble, remember that praying through is what to do instead of giving up.

I grew up on a cattle ranch in western South Dakota. Before we saddled a horse, we would put on a saddle blanket to protect the horse's back during the long ride. This kept saddle sores from forming. How silly it would be to saddle and ride a horse with no saddle blanket. Even sillier, however, would be to put a saddle blanket on the poor horse in the evening after his back was already rubbed raw from being ridden during the day without proper padding.

In the same way, we all are saddled and ridden by the responsibilities of our day. By having a good time of morning prayer first, it is as if we've put on a saddle blanket. When the weight of responsibilities comes on us we are padded by the peace we found in morning prayer. Many, however, do not pray in the morning. They only say a prayer before bedtime. So these believers are already rubbed raw by the friction of the day's stresses. Their evening prayer does not protect them from what's already happened. It is as if they padded themselves too late.

In 1996, when I was pastoring in Omaha, I went through a wrenching church split. The trouble lasted almost six months. It was an all-out attack of the devil to destroy me. Five different letters were sent out to my entire congregation calling me all kinds of names and making all kinds of accusations. To keep from giving up, I had morning prayer meetings from 4:30 a.m. to 7:30 a.m. Monday through Friday, and from 7:00 a.m. to 9:00 a.m. on Saturday. I did this for approximately six months. One morning, I was meditating on God's Word and I found a verse that gave me hope. "Thou dost hide them in the secret place of Thy presence from the conspiracies of man; Thou dost keep them secretly in a shelter from the strife of tongues" (Ps. 31:20, NAS).

When I saw this I prayed, "Oh God. This is what I need. Please hide me in the secret place of Your presence from the conspiracies of men. Hide me in this special shelter from the strife of tongues." Immediately God spoke to me, *I will if you will stay out of it.* He meant that I could choose to be in the strife of tongues or be hidden away from it. I could not be in both places. I knew that if I refused to say bad things about those who were saying bad things about me I could be hidden in this secret place in God. I followed that strategy and God helped me.

That was another example of praying through. I was in prayer from 4:30 a.m. to 7:30 a.m., and in one of those meetings I prayed through, and I heard from God. I entered the arena of God's peace and stayed in it, though Satan baited me to come out into the strife that was all around me. Because I kept my spirit sweet, I passed the test. When that test was completed I knew God was going to send me all around America to teach Christians the necessity of walking in love and having a sweet spirit.

George Mueller, the apostle of prayer, provided for two thousand orphans and refused to use common fund-raising techniques. He only used prayer because he wanted to show the world that God answers prayer. His method was to read the Bible on his knees for one hour. Then, having received faith from God's Word, he gave God his petitions in the next hour and saw the miraculous provision of the Almighty.

Friend, you do not have to quit. The enemy may have you surrounded. The foes may be numerous. The situation may be preposterous, outrageously stacked in the devil's favor. The devil may be at your door demanding you sign a document of surrender. But you, child of God, can pray through.

Chapter 3

EXAMINE YOUR THOUGHTS AND GET GOD'S THOUGHTS

We take captive every thought
to make it obedient to Christ.
—2 Corinthians 10:5—

When you are considering giving up, when quitting looks like the only option, it is always because you are thinking thoughts from the devil. Satan comes to steal, kill, and destroy. (See John 10:10.) He attacks by sending thoughts to your mind with the intention of stealing your faith, killing your hope, and destroying your morale. Your ability to continue obeying God, your perseverance, will be in direct proportion to how you guard and control your thoughts.

I fly on airplanes a lot as I travel back and forth across America. Each airport has security checkpoints. I have to present photo I.D., my boarding pass, and walk through a metal detector. These security measures were put into place to prevent terrorists from hijacking an airliner. There are still many terrorists out there who would do exactly that if we let them. However, now we are guarding our airports.

But what about our minds? Do you have any security checkpoints that ask your thoughts for I.D. and boarding passes? If you let just any old thought on board your mind, your life is going to be hijacked by satanic thoughts and plunged into destruction. The average Christian has almost no security system in place to guard their minds from evil thoughts. You must make your thoughts pass through a screening process. If these thoughts are not good thoughts, well behaved and helpful, then do not allow them into your mind.

It is easy to spot thoughts from Satan. They are always mad, bad, or sad. God is not the author of those thoughts. No matter how true the thought may seem, if it is mad, bad, or sad do not let it on board. You must take full responsibility for what thoughts you allow to take a seat on your mental airplane. Airlines give seats to paying customers. Why give a seat to a thought that is going to cost you dearly? Why not reserve all the space in your mind for thoughts that are going to profit you in some way?

The apostle Paul had great perseverance in large part because he carefully chose his thoughts. "Finally, brothers, whatever is true, whatever is noble, whatever is right, whatever is pure, whatever is lovely, whatever is admirable— if anything is excellent or praiseworthy—think about such things" (Phil. 4:8).

God wants us to intentionally search for, find, and recruit the very best thoughts to occupy our thinking. Our thought selection process should not be random or accidental. The wise intentionally go looking for excellent thoughts in God's Word and retain them. They also pray for God to speak original thoughts to them. They keep on asking until they have a collection of wonderful thoughts given first to them, thoughts they can then share to benefit others. They also read books and are always on the lookout for those key thoughts they want to put in their minds. They know that if their minds are filled with good thoughts, they will have profitable lives.

Profitable airlines want to fly with every seat filled, not with empty seats. Many Christians are flying with a lot of empty seats on their mental airplanes. There may not be a bunch of terrible thoughts on board, but neither are there a lot of good thoughts. There are just empty seats—a mostly blank mind going, "Duuhhh." Friend, we can do better than that.

Many mad, bad, or sad thoughts may already be in your mind. The plot to hijack your life may be well underway. They may have been on board for a long time and may have already

Can you find the terrorist thoughts on board this "Mental Airplane"? They'll hijack this life unless they are taken captive.

caused you a lot of damage and hindrance, if not destruction. To get them off, you first need to identify them. Then you will need a bouncer-type thought, something bigger and stronger that comes from God. God's thoughts can subdue and arrest mad, bad, and sad thoughts and take them captive.

Throughout my adult life, I have prayed one prayer over and over, "Dear Lord, please give me one of Your thoughts. Just one thought from You and I am out of this jam." That's a truly dynamic prayer, one you can pray often. I want to share with you some of the original thoughts God gave just to me, to first help me and equip me to help many others.

In 1982, one year after I founded a church in Omaha, one of my church ladies told me about a strange vision God gave her. In the vision, I was preaching to a group of people when many of them became very angry at me. She was amazed at the intensity of their anger. "They rushed at you gnashing their teeth," she said. "But you just rose up on the air and continued to preach to them and they couldn't harm you." I hoped her vision was false. How could I rise up in the air to continue to preach? I forgot about it.

From 1991 to 1993, I became heavily involved in deliverance ministry and got out of balance. I held some false assumptions, and because of them, I sinned ignorantly (not willfully). God helped me untangle the mess, and one Sunday I apologized to the church for my errors. I majored on warfare and minored on worship. I also majored on exposing the devil and minored on revealing Christ. I repented and asked God, my congregation, my radio audience, and many individuals to forgive me.

That day, as I promised my church that I would major on worship and revealing Christ and minor on warfare and revealing the devil, a young prophet in our church heard the rattling of chains. He looked to the double doors of our sanctuary and saw two doors in the spirit right above them.

Both disappeared as I repented, but one small door was left. In his vision, he then saw a dragon insert it's head through the small door. It tried to bite people but couldn't, and it was enraged that it could no longer enter the church. From his vision I realized that I had opened two doors for the devil by my wrong emphasis. The young man said the third door, the small one, represented the unforgiveness of the people. If they forgave me, the door would close. If not, it would remain as an access for the devil.

A few weeks later, this young man had a second vision. The Spirit of God took him in a vision into that small door. A tunnel was attached to it. In the tunnel, evil spirits were preparing for war, forging knives, spears, and swords and sharpening them. His words were ominous, "They are preparing to attack you, Wes. All those weapons were being made just to harm you. The evil spirits plan to attack and they'll come through that door of unforgiveness unless it is closed." He said the tunnel opened on the other end to a red city of spirits who were all red in color and that an invasion was planned. I knew the red color represented raging anger and that a city of such spirits meant there would be a large number in the invasion force. I didn't hope this vision was false. I knew it was true. I hoped that I could get the people to forgive me so that such an invasion would never happen. About three years after that young man's second vision I fired a staff member. Then all hell broke loose. Many people became furious with me and the level of rage was incredible—plus it kept spreading to more people. The words spoken against me were like verbal swords, spears, and knives.

The remembrance of those three visions helped me believe that I was enduring an attack by the enemy rather than the judgment of God. They kept me from giving up in despair. I believe the experience was something the devil meant for evil but God meant for good. It gave me great compassion for pastors.

Previously, I would have had judgmental thoughts about the leadership ability of pastors going through such things. After it was all over, I resigned and traveled as an evangelist. But I kept my radio program in Omaha for another year. That first vision had said, "You rose up in the air and continued to preach to them." I did rise up in courage, stayed in the ministry, and preached "on the air" (radio). I got through this trial by fire because I practiced these principles of perseverance.

While this crisis was still raging, I was doing my best to "pray through" and a few joined me in daily morning prayer meetings. But one morning I was all alone.

One morning, I was feeling really sad that so many who had once loved me now hated me. It is never right to think sad thoughts, but it was a fact. Many who had loved me now hated me. The thought was true—but it was sad. It was true but not excellent, noble, or praiseworthy. Should I have given it a seat in my mind? I held the thought for questioning and appealed to God for His thoughts and perspective on the subject.

Then God spoke to me and asked, *Why did Joseph's brothers hate him?* I spoke out loud, "They hated him because his father loved him more." (See Genesis 37.) Then God expanded on that and understanding flooded my heart and mind. Joseph was seventeen-years-old and had been the first son of Jacob's wife Rachel, who died giving birth to Benjamin. Jacob was very attached to Joseph and had made him a coat of many colors. His half-brothers hated him although he had not done anything wrong to any of them.

God continued to speak to my heart, *I love all My children equally when it comes to acceptance. But My approval—My approving love—is reserved for those who obey Me. When one of my children obeys me, I give that child special anointings that the others do not have. Some of these children then become jealous and hateful of the child who is clothed in the many-colored robe of special anointing.* (See John 14:21–23.)

Then I dared to think it through a bit more, and a thought came to me that brought me life, *What if the brethren hate me because my Father loves me more? What if I have obeyed Him enough to have His approval? What if the anointings He has given me are like that coat of many colors, provoking jealousy in the brethren who have not been as obedient as me?* Another thought said, *Yeah, well what if all this is happening because you are just a big jerk and have made stupid leadership errors?*

I had a choice to make. I could give a seat to the thought, *Look how many of the brethren hate you,* or seat the thought, *I must be doing something wrong or this would not be happening.* But, if I wanted to, I could give a seat to the thought, *Maybe the Father is giving me more of His approving love. Maybe this is happening because my Father loves me more.* One thought was true, but very sad. One thought was very demoralizing and I hoped it wasn't true. I did not think it was. Just one thought was very encouraging, but was it true?

Perhaps people were mad at me because I should have handled the situation differently. I knew my heart, and how hard I tried to please God in every way all day long. I could also feel the holy fire of God's anointing burning inside me— a tangible fire in my hands and often in my feet. I often felt the mantle of a teaching anointing upon me that would so clothe me my hands would tremble under the weight of it. There was no question about it, I did have anointings that others did not have.

I made my choice. I would go around thinking how much my Father loved me instead of how much my brothers hated me. As soon as I seated that encouraging thought and denied boarding privileges to the sad thoughts I felt so much better. I had hope and courage once again. It is not hard to persevere in obedience when you are thinking, *Wow. My Father really loves me.* It is hard to keep going if your main thought is, *Wow. Look at how many people who used to love me now hate me.* Friend, you are responsible for what type of thoughts occupy your mind. You must choose the right ones. The Holy Spirit can give you these excellent thoughts direct from His mind or help you find them as you read God's Word and good books.

My own convert, and personal friend, Dr. Pat Burgess once had a vision of three men railing at him and shaking their fingers at him. These three men were causing him a lot of trouble in the church he pastored. In the vision, God cut off the first joint in the finger each one was pointing at Pat. The first week after the vision one of those men literally cut off the end of his finger in an accident with a lawn mower. The next week the second man lost the end of his finger when he was using a hedge trimmer. Pat called the third man and warned him what was going to happen to him if he did not repent. That man did repent and was spared the loss of his finger.

Then I considered what some men had done to me in my church. I was thinking, *God, they've done many more damaging things—would not it be appropriate it you cut off their heads?* Okay, profile that thought. What kind of thought is that? Is it mad? Is it sad? Is it bad? It is all three, yet I needed some help to get it taken captive, so I asked God for one of His thoughts.

He spoke, *What if I had judged Joseph's brothers?* I knew the story well. Joseph had been sold as a slave by his jealous brothers. But by God's preordained plan he was later exalted to the right hand of Pharaoh, king of Egypt. When famine came to Canaan and Egypt Joseph's brothers came to Egypt to buy food. Joseph was in charge of the granaries of Egypt so his brothers appeared before him. Something like seventeen years had passed. They all looked healthy. None were missing any body parts.

I began to imagine how different it could have been if God

had judged Joseph's brothers. I imagined one mangled brother standing before Joseph. Joseph would have said, "Do not you have a bunch of other brothers?" The guy would have said, "Well, I did, but we sold our half-brother Joseph as a slave—and God punished us. Lightening struck two of my brothers. One brother died from a snakebite. A bull gored another brother to death. Robbers killed two more brothers. One brother died of a plague, and a camel kicked the head off of another brother. A hailstone killed one brother and a boulder rolled off a cliff and crushed me. I lived, but I am in constant pain. We never should have sold our brother as a slave."

I thought, *Would Joseph have shouted, "Oh, hallelujah. Praise the Lord. I have been vindicated."* I did not think so. Instead of that gory scenario, God had kept them all alive for seventeen years and brought about a great reconciliation. Joseph enjoyed providing for them and once again they were a big family.

Then God spoke a second time, *Would you like a Joseph miracle?* I said, "That would be a lot better, wouldn't it? Yes. I would like a Joseph miracle." So instead of giving a seat to a wish for vengeance, I gave a seat to a hopeful thought of future reconciliation. Later, I did have a wonderful reconciliation miracle with most of the brethren and I am still hoping for a Joseph style miracle with the remainder.

Satan really tried hard to get me wishing for judgment to fall on those who had caused me the most trouble. A thought kept coming to me, *Would not it be right and just for God to judge them?* It is not so easy to get rid of a thought that is buzzing around like a summer fly intent on fellowshiping with you. I needed another thought from God in order to take captive this pesky thought that Satan was trying over and over again to implant in my mind. I kept asking God, "What's the right way to think about this? How do I answer this nagging question?"

Then God showed me a great truth. When the martyr Stephen was being stoned he cried out, "Lord, do not hold this sin against them" (Acts 7:60). Then he died. He did not go home to his family that night. His children never saw their dad alive on earth again. His young wife was widowed. There was a lot of pain, and Saul of Tarsus, the young Sanhedrin member who was in charge of the stoning, was the focal point of the guilt.

But Stephen had virtually entrusted his pain into God's hands and had asked that it not be used as a justification for judgment, but rather that his pain would be turned into revelations of God's love. So Saul became the focal point of divine mercy.

Saul was going to Damascus to arrest more Christians when a light from heaven struck him to the ground. If it had been a bolt of God's wrath it could have fried him like a strip of bacon on a griddle! Nothing left but a grease spot. Instead, the light from heaven turned him into an apostle.

Then God made me understand that if I entrusted all my pain into His hand and asked God to turn it into revelations of mercy instead of judgment I just might get an apostle out of the deal. That's when He asked me, *Do you want a grease spot or an apostle?* I said, "I would rather have an apostle." So I gave God all my pain and gave Him the legal right to give revelations of divine mercy to those who weren't seeking it.

I was able to recover from the trauma of that terrible church split because I gave seating assignments only to the thoughts that came from God. I went around thinking, *My pain will not be wasted. It has been invested. I am believing for an apostle, not a grease spot. I am looking forward to a Joseph style miracle.* Starting in January of 1997, I began traveling America holding meetings in churches and teaching Christians how to keep their spirits sweet. I had been tested severely, but I had refused to think bitter, angry, self-pitying, vengeful thoughts. After the test, God had promoted me to reach many more than I did while pastoring.

In that first year of traveling, 178 people were baptized in the Holy Spirit in my meetings through the laying on of my hands. That was a greater number than had received the Spirit through my ministry in fifteen years of pastoring. What Satan intended for evil God had intended for good:

> "For my thoughts are not your thoughts, neither are your ways my ways," declares the LORD. "As the heavens are higher than the earth, so are my ways higher than your ways and my thoughts than your thoughts. As the rain and the snow come down from heaven, and do not return to it without watering the earth and making it bud and flourish, so that it yields seed for the sower and bread for the eater, so is my word that goes out from my mouth: it will not return to me empty, but will accomplish what I desire and achieve the purpose for which I sent it."
> —ISAIAH 55:8–11

God is *not* saying, *My thoughts are higher than your thoughts and I am not going to share them, nah, nah, nah.* He is saying, *My thoughts are way better than yours and they will make your life bud, blossom, and bear fruit. Do not you want me to share them with you? Just ask for them. I want you to desire them. I want to give them to you.*

Will you ask for them? Will you search for them? Will you collect them? If you do, you will be able to persist in obedience and experience great victories and intimacy with God as a result.

Years ago God showed me there were five steps to life and five steps to death. They are the same steps, but you can take them up or down. They are: 1. exposure, 2. tolerance, 3. meditation, 4. tasting, and 5. indulgence.

It is possible for a Christian to fall down these steps rather quickly. Longevity in ministry depends upon living a holy life. A holy life is impossible if we are meditating on various sins and trying not to do them. It all depends where we draw the line against sin.

Suppose a spiritual leader is working on a computer and accidentally brings up a pornographic Web site. He's exposed to the things of the devil. If he stares at this and does not get out of that screen, he will be guilty of tolerating sin. That kind of tolerance is evil. (See Revelation 2:20.)

> Nevertheless, I have this against you: you tolerate that woman Jezebel, who calls herself a prophetess. By her teaching, she misleads my servants into sexual immorality and the eating of food sacrificed to idols.
> —REVELATION 12:20

People soon meditate on what they tolerate. This is a spiritual law, and one of the main reasons Satan is pushing his brand of "tolerance" so heavily in the American school system and society in general.

When a man constantly meditates on that Web site, there will be a strong pull to go back to it, willfully. If he goes back to that site, he will be tasting the cup of sin. "You cannot drink the cup of the Lord and the cup of demons too" (1 Cor. 10:21). If he does not repent of this, but chooses to continually indulge his flesh, he will become addicted and be bound with a demonic chain. He will be taken captive to do the devil's will. God's grace will not cover rebellion. "If we deliberately keep on sinning after we have received the knowledge of the truth, no sacrifice for sins is left, but only a fearful expectation of judgment and of raging fire that will consume the enemies of God" (Heb. 10:26–27).

In the spiritual realm, when we are exposed to sin, a little thread of oppression is wrapped around us. If we tolerate that exposure and continue to look at it, the oppression becomes like a string. If we meditate on evil, the oppression is strengthened and becomes like twine. If we willfully "taste" of the sin, the oppression becomes a "cord of iniquity." "The evil deeds of a wicked man ensnare him; the cords of his sin hold him fast" (Prov. 5:22). Willful indulgence becomes a chain of demonic bondage. "Now stop your mocking, or your chains will become heavier" (Isa. 28:22).

Many spiritual leaders and their followers as well have drawn the line against sin in the wrong place. They are trying not to taste it. Meanwhile they have allowed themselves to be exposed to it, they've tolerated it, and they are thinking about doing it, while trying to resist. They are three steps down the stairway to death. These are the people who say, "It is hard to live for the Lord." Of course it is hard, when you are three steps down on the stairway to death.

How much better to draw the line against sin before exposure and do your best to avoid exposure to worldly and perverse things? If we are accidentally exposed we should snap that thread of spiritual oppression by refusing to tolerate it. Turn to another channel quickly, turn the computer off, or get out of the store that is selling the alluring images.

To really live in holiness we must expose ourselves to the things of God on a daily basis. If we do this we are moving up the stairway of life. We must tolerate the correction of God's Word. We must meditate on God's Word day and night so we can be careful to do it and make our way prosperous and successful. (See Joshua 1:9.) We must taste and see that the Lord is good. (See Psalm 34:8.) Then we will walk in the Spirit, indulging in the things of God and we will be ten steps away from life-destroying addictions. "This I say then, Walk in the Spirit, and ye shall not fulfill the lust of the flesh" (Gal. 5:16, KJV).

Taking every thought captive involves taking images captive—or avoiding bad images in the first place. "Casting down imaginations, and every high thing that exalteth itself against the knowledge of God, and bringing into captivity every thought to the obedience of Christ" (2 Cor. 10:5, KJV).

We must cast out the images that would lure us into sin and avoid getting these images into our heads. It is easy to live for God when we are walking in the Spirit, away from bondage. God wants us to indulge in the good things of God and delight in the fellowship of the Holy Spirit. We should expose ourselves daily to God's Word, allow its correction, meditate on it, and taste that the Lord is good. Then, we should indulge in the sweet fellowship of the Holy Spirit.

Take responsibility for the thoughts you think and the images on which you meditate. Choose only the finest and you will be strengthened to overcome the world, the flesh, and the devil.

Chapter 4

RESIST SATAN'S
EVALUATIONS

*Be self-controlled and alert. Your enemy
the devil prowls around like a roaring lion
looking for someone to devour. Resist him,
standing firm in the faith.*
—1 Peter 5:8–9—

If Satan came around dressed in a red suit, holding a pitch-
fork, and offering some salacious temptation, the average
Christian *would* resist him. But most are not prepared to resist
Satan when he grades their spiritual performance and hands
them the report card through some close relative, friend, or
church member. If the believer accepts Satan's evaluation as
truth, their spiritual stride will be thrown off and they will
stumble. Every athlete needs a performance coach who gives
him or her a true evaluation of their performance so they can
adjust appropriately. How often would they win if they were
accepting advice from an enemy coach? That is exactly what is
happening to many Christians.

Satan tried this tactic repeatedly and unsuccessfully on
David just prior to David's amazing victory over Goliath.
The prophet Samuel had anointed David to be the future

king in the presence of his seven brothers when David was only a teenager. Of the oldest brother, the Spirit of God told Samuel, "Do not consider his appearance or his height, for I have rejected him. The LORD does not look at the things man looks at. Man looks at the outward appearance, but the LORD looks at the heart" (1 Sam. 16:7). Keep that in mind. God had already evaluated David as having a better heart attitude than his older brother.

David's father sent him to see how his four oldest brothers were faring. They were with King Saul, supposedly fighting the Philistines. When David arrived he found them in a forty-day standoff with the enemy. Just then, the Philistine champion, Goliath, a giant nearly ten feet tall came out and made his challenge. David watched the men of Israel back up in fear. He heard the men saying that King Saul would give great rewards to the man who would kill this Philistine. David asked the men standing near him, "What will be done for the man who kills this Philistine and removes this disgrace from Israel? Who is this uncircumcised Philistine that he should defy the armies of the living God?" (1 Sam. 17:26).

David's oldest brother heard this and burned with anger. Satan used him to hand David a report card on his spiritual status. "Why have you come down here? And with whom did you leave those few sheep in the desert? I know how conceited you are and how wicked your heart is; you came down only to watch the battle" (1 Sam. 17:28).

Wow. His own brother was saying, "You are insignificant. You only watch a *few* sheep. You are irresponsible. You probably did not leave them with anyone. You are wicked and conceited. You are also completely inadequate to do anything more than to just sit and watch." If David had believed even a portion of that he never would have volunteered. Please note, it was David's brother who had the wicked and conceited heart and who had been cowardly for forty days, only watching the giant and not fighting. The spiritual plank in his eye was superimposed over David so that it looked as if it was in David's eye. Hypocrites are great at accusing pure hearted people of having the same spiritual problems they have but are unaware of.

David resisted Satan's evaluation that came through his own brother and soon stood before the king to volunteer for battle. Immediately Satan spoke through King Saul, "You are not able to go out against this Philistine and fight him; you are only a boy, and he has been a fighting man from his youth" (1 Sam. 17:33). What if David had accepted this evaluation as truth? He would have said, "That's right. I am too little. He's too big. I am not trained. He's got years and years of training." He never would have gone forth to the battle. David did not listen to that. He was listening to his own coach, the Holy Spirit so he went forth to meet the giant.

The devil wants to tell you, "You are only a woman. Women cannot do anything great," or, "You are over fifty. It is too late for you," or, "You are bald. Teenagers will not listen to a bald-headed man." Do not listen. Resist him. It is not about us. The devil wants to make us self conscious or self-focused so that our faith is hindered.

Satan spoke through Goliath. As David approached him he scoffed, "Am I a dog, that you come at me with sticks?" (1 Sam. 17:43). The Philistine cursed David in an attack against David's mind. The devil was saying, "You are in way over your head, boy. You are out of your mind. What in the world are you doing out here?"

If David had agreed with that and paused to second-guess himself, a sixteen-pound spearhead would have gone through him like a Civil War cannonball. Yet, David was victorious over Goliath and the whole Philistine army. Satan's three efforts to stop this cycle of success failed because David wasn't listening to any coach but the Holy Spirit. God won a great victory through him and wants to triumph through you, too. Satan is going to try to prevent this by speaking through people he has influence over. David's jealous brother, backslidden King Saul, and blasphemous Goliath were all easy puppets for Satan to use.

Jesus tells all of us to first take the planks out of our own eyes so we can see clearly to take specks out of the eyes of others. (See Luke 6:42.) People who still have planks in their own eyes are handy tools for Satan. Because their viewpoints are so distorted, he can easily influence them to speak what he wants said. I learned the hard way never to let the devil evaluate me.

When I pastored in Omaha I was invited to speak at Christ For The Nations, a large Bible college in Dallas, Texas. That week the Spirit of God used me in a great way and I came home elated and on a spiritual high. When I got home, my board asked for a meeting with me. One of them had received a prophecy for me.

It said, "You are not listening to me and because you are not listening to me I am going to destroy this church within a year." It came through one of my brothers who seemed to have a sweet spirit. I accepted this word as coming from God. It broke my heart. I wept there before the board, my nose running profusely in my brokenness. I asked them, "Do any of you have any examples of how I have not listened to God?" None of them had anything to say. So I gave them copies of the prophecy and sent them home to pray about it. I asked them to call me if they could shed some light on how I might obey God better.

After they left, I felt completely cut off from God. I had been seeking Him three hours-a-day every weekday morning.

How could He say to me, _You are not listening._ There was no use in trying anymore. I was dead inside. I told God, "If there were two god's right now, I would go check out the other god." It was as if He had spit on me. (Spiritually, I had been spit on, but not by God.)

I tried to record my radio broadcast that Monday but gave up after the first fifteen minutes and went home. One lady heard that broadcast and called me saying, "Brother Wes, what has happened to you?" She was crying because I sounded so wiped out. Then I looked closely at the prophecy. Part of it said, "I have given you the board to direct you and you are not listening to the board so you are not listening to Me." All of a sudden I realized the prophecy had a scriptural error in it. God gave me the Holy Spirit to indwell me and guide me from within. God would never give men to do what His own Spirit had been given to do.

As soon as I said, "This prophecy is not from God," my anointing returned. I knew God wasn't mad at me. This was the devil speaking through a brother who's own viewpoint was distorted. Believing that demonic prophecy had been like swallowing broken glass. It had torn me up inside. From then on, I have been careful not to accept words that do not bear witness with my spirit. God's rebukes and corrections always have been delightfully frank and truthful, but have always pulled me close to His heart. I love God's correction. But I do not take any lip off the devil. His words are condemning and will push you away from God if you believe them. You must never listen to Satan's evaluations and viewpoints.

I rejected that demonic prophecy with such force I also rejected the brother who gave it. As I have matured I have gotten better at just ignoring words like that while continuing to show love to the people who speak them. We have to be bigger. We have to know who we are and be secure in that even when others are judging us as being evil.

After a few years, I made contact with that brother again. He actually typeset one of my books for free and did a few other graphic art jobs for me. Then about twelve years after his first prophecy I went to see him one day and he said, "I have got another prophecy for you." It was more of the same, but this time I did not tell him I rejected it. Instead, I bought him a book about the ministry of a prophet. It had helpful information about how prophetic people can listen to wrong spirits if they are not careful. I thought perhaps it would help him escape from his deception. Privately, I forgave him and prayed for him, but never said one word to him about the prophecy.

This second prophecy said God was going to remove me from the ministry. It had the trademark of Satan—condemnation—running all through it. The year I was supposed to be removed from the ministry was the greatest year of ministry to that point in my life. A total of 178 people were baptized in the Holy Spirit in my meetings. If I had allowed the devil to evaluate me, I would have quit. Instead, I saw God move in marvelous ways in my meetings.

Over the years, I have had some really choice zingers spoken to me. One lady said, "I saw a vision of a wrecking ball hitting your church and destroying it. God said He'd destroy your church because you are a bribe taker." She thought her husband was bribing me to say part of their marriage problem was her fault. Another lady was angry at me when her husband went to jail for selling drugs. She said, "You do not have a relationship with anybody, not even God." One man wrote me, "You make converts only to yourself, not Jesus Christ. I can say without fear of contradiction—you will not inherit the kingdom of God."

Friend, if you are called to do something great for God,

you can be sure that Satan will try to get you to quit obeying God. He will just speak things like this through others, and if you believe it—you will quit. If you do not believe it but get bitter, angry, or hurt, you will probably quit or become ineffective. If you make a big deal out of it, you will go around thinking about it all day long and have your focus shifted from what God is doing to what the devil did.

If you make the most of your call to fellowship with Christ, then God will choose you for special assignments. Jesus said, "For many are called, but few are chosen," (Matt. 22:14, NKJV). When you get chosen and others do not they will speak things to you like David's oldest brother spoke to him. You must ignore these words and love these brethren.

Just knowing that Satan wants to influence the way we perceive ourselves and our situations should cause us to depend even more upon the Spirit of Truth. If things seem really bad to us, we should ask the Holy Spirit if our way of seeing things has been tampered with. Often it has.

Once I was feeling terrible about myself. It seemed as if a scale from zero to ten was upon my chest and the arrow of value had slid down to zero. I prayed, "Lord, I feel so bad about myself. I do not think You want me to feel like a zero, but I do not think You want me to feel like I am a ten, the grandest tiger in the jungle. Just where on the scale do You want the arrow to be?" He spoke firmly to me, *Turn that arrow around and focus on Me.*

Self-focus puts us at a disadvantage, no matter where we see the arrow of value pointing. If we are self-focused our self-image will be distorted into one of the awful three—self-hatred, mediocrity, or an arrogant air of superiority. *Supernatural faith is not going to come from any form of self-focus.*

Go back to the story of David and Goliath. David's focus was not on himself at all. From the get-go his words show that his total focus was upon the Lord. "Who is this uncircumcised Philistine that he should defy the armies of the living God?" (1 Sam. 17:26). Satan knew this young man would be incredibly dangerous. He had to get David's focus off the Lord and onto himself. He slammed David with insults against his character, body, and mind but as the battle commenced, David's words were still full of supernatural faith that came from total dependence and focus upon God.

> David said to the Philistine, "You come against me with sword and spear and javelin, but I come against you in the name of the LORD Almighty, the God of the armies of Israel, whom you have defied. This day the LORD will hand you over to me, and I'll strike you down and cut off your head. Today I will give the carcasses of the Philistine army to the birds of the air and the beasts of the earth, and the whole world will know that there is a God in Israel. All those gathered here will know that it is not by sword or spear that the LORD saves; for the battle is the LORD's, and he will give all of you into our hands."
>
> —1 SAMUEL 17:45–47

The prophet Elijah had a meltdown of courage when Queen Jezebel promised to have him murdered. (See 1 Kings 19.) The situation looked totally hopeless, as if he was the only remaining servant of the Lord. "Lord, they have killed your prophets and torn down your altars; I am the only one left, and they are trying to kill me " (Rom. 11:3). The situation was actually seven thousand times better than Elijah was perceiving it. Good thing for him that God straightened this out by saying, "I have reserved for myself seven thousand who have not bowed the knee to Baal" (Romans 11:4).

No doubt Satan had been distorting Elijah's perception of

the situation to make it look so bad he would give up obeying God. But after the Holy Spirit showed him what things looked like from God's viewpoint, Elijah's faith was unstoppable. When the wicked king of Israel sent a small army to arrest him, Elijah called fire down from heaven upon them.

We need to get in a habit of asking God what things look like from His perspective. When I pastored in Omaha I went through many incredibly difficult times. Attacks of all kinds had come against the church and we weren't growing anymore. Thoughts were bombarding my mind saying, *You are not advancing. Your advance has stalled. You have failed.* I had to agree that it looked that way. But I had developed a habit of not trusting my own perceptions and I had learned to especially doubt any voice that spoke discouragement to me. So I asked the Lord for His take on the situation.

He completely surprised me. He said, *You are not in an advance. You are in a 'stand.' A stand is a defensive battle where the enemy's advance is stopped by the courage of the defenders. You have held your ground in a successful stand against the enemy's advance. It is his advance that has stalled. He's the one who is not advancing anymore.* Then God showed me that often the whole tide of a war is turned when a successful stand is made. The battle of Gettysburg was a Union stand against the advance of General Lee and the Confederate army. The Battle of Britain was a defensive stand against the advance of Hitler's air force. In each case, the tide of the war was turned by a courageous stand.

I had been feeling like a failure when in fact my Father was pleased with me. The reality of the situation was just the opposite of what Satan was saying. His advance had been stopped. He had failed. The tide of the battle had been turned in my favor. But that did not stop him from spinning the situation to make it look like I was the failure. When God congratulated me on making a successful stand, I found new courage and have been advancing on the enemy ever since.

In Revelation 2 and 3, Jesus spoke to seven churches. He talked to them about the three different kinds of sin. Three churches were in sins of omission, Satan's favorite kind of sin, because people rarely realize they are in it. Two churches were committing sins of commission—idolatry and immorality. Two churches were pure, but were suffering from the sins of others who came against them—persecution.

Satan doesn't like to waste persecution because if he persecutes lukewarm people it could push them into closer dependence upon the Lord and end up making them stronger. Now suppose a pastor is a good, kind man who is morally pure and works hard in the ministry. Satan cannot trap this righteous man in any sin of omission or sin of commission. Daniel was a man like that. The only kind of sin the devil could use against him was the sins of others—persecution. As Daniel was thrown into the lion's den for no sin of his own, so the godly pastor will be attacked sooner or later.

You must qualify to be persecuted. Paul wrote, "Yea, and all that will live godly in Christ Jesus shall suffer persecution" (2 Tim. 3:12, KJV). That's why Jesus said, "Blessed are you when people insult you, persecute you, and falsely say all kinds of evil against you because of me. Rejoice and be glad, because great is your reward in heaven, for in the same way they persecuted the prophets who were before you" (Matt. 5:11–12).

When people in the church mistreat a godly pastor, the devil says to that minister, "None of this would be happening to you if you were a good leader. Your leadership ability is so bad you should quit and let someone else have a try. You've let this get out of hand. It just proves you are unworthy to be in the ministry." Remember, we must resist Satan's evaluation of the situations we are in. Why did Cain kill Abel? Was Abel a bad communicator? Was he a bad leader? Did he sin against Cain? No! He was murdered because he was righteous and his brother, Cain, was evil! (See 1 John 3:12.)

If a minister lives above sins of omission and commission the only thing Satan has to use against him or her will be the sins of others. The devil hopes that when the baseless attacks come, persecuted people will either get bitter and retaliate and commit sins of commission or perhaps they will get so discouraged they'll quit and move into sins of omission.

Just remember that you have to qualify to be persecuted, and if you are indeed a man or woman of God, you will be persecuted. How you view it will determine whether or not you survive it. If you allow yourself to view it through the devil's lenses you'll be wiped out. You must ask God to help you properly evaluate the situation and see it from His perspective. If you can see it as God does, you'll rejoice about the great heavenly reward that is piling up for you. You can say, "Wow. My enemies are doing all the work and I'm getting all the rewards! Cool!"

A pastor friend of mine shared with me that for the entire thirty years he had been in the ministry, he constantly felt unworthy to pastor because he was not musical like other ministers. He noticed now many pastors could play instruments and sing. The devil evaluated him as being unfit for ministry. My friend hadn't given up, but his faith had been hindered because this thought turned his focus on himself instead of God.

When he confessed to me he'd never felt worthy to be a pastor because of his lack of musical ability I immediately asked, "Are you one of these guys who can organize a crew of men, take them to Mexico, and build a church?"

"Oh, yes," he said. "I have done that many times. I can

even draw up the architectural plans." I told him, "Brother, I cannot even pound a nail in straight. But I can write a song."

We talked further and he realized God had given him all the leadership gifts he needed to do what he was called to do. The next night he said publicly, "I am never going to let Satan evaluate me again." He had discovered one of the perseverance secrets of the apostles—resisting Satan's evaluations and viewpoints.

Chapter 5

MAKE A DEEPER COMMITMENT TO GOD

Therefore, holy brothers, who share in the heavenly calling, fix your thoughts on Jesus, the apostle and high priest whom we confess.
—Hebrews 3:1—

Jesus is the divine Son of God, but He ministered on earth as a Man anointed by the Holy Spirit, filling all five of the ministry roles as an Apostle, Prophet, Evangelist, Pastor, and Teacher. He set an example, not only for other full-time ministers, but for every Christian. He perfectly modeled one of the most important perseverance techniques for spiritual champions—making a deeper commitment to God when at His lowest point emotionally.

Then Jesus went with His disciples to a place called Gethsemane, and He said to them, "Sit here while I go over there and pray" (Matt. 26:36). He took Peter and the two sons of Zebedee along with Him, and He began to be sorrowful and troubled. Then He said to them, "My soul is overwhelmed with sorrow to the point of death. Stay here and keep watch with me" (Matt. 26: 38).

If you are sorrowful, troubled, and overwhelmed, it may

seem like giving up the pursuit of obedience is completely justified. When every fuel gauge in your brain, body, and emotions are all saying, "Your strength is completely gone," it seems like coasting to a stop is inevitable. In times like this, a true spiritual champion does not find an excuse to quit. Rather, he or she finds a way to gain new strength and complete their assignment from God.

At the lowest emotional point of Jesus' earthly life, He made His deepest commitment to do God's will. "'Father, if you are willing, take this cup from me; yet not my will, but yours be done.' An angel from heaven appeared to him and strengthened him" (Luke 22:42–43).

Physically, mentally, and emotionally, it appeared that Jesus did not have the strength to keep on obeying. Nevertheless, He made an all-out commitment to do God's will—strength or no strength. When this commitment was made, God immediately sent an angel to give Him that extra needed strength.

When it seems impossible to continue, the typical believer says, "Lord, I cannot commit to doing Your will unless You first send an angel to strengthen me." God says, *You first make the commitment to do My will, and then I will send the angel.* This is a great principle of perseverance. The angel comes with the strength *after* you make an all-out commitment to do God's will.

Before you quit obeying God, remember that someday you will stand before the judgment seat of Christ. Imagine saying to Him, "Jesus, I had to quit because I just could not go on. I ran out of strength physically, mentally, and emotionally. Surely You understand, don't You?" He's going to say, "I ran out of strength, too, but I did not quit. I made a deeper commitment to God and received new strength from my Father." *There are no acceptable excuses for failing to persevere in obedience to God.*

Luke 22:42   Luke 22:43

The angel comes to strengthen us AFTER we make our deepest commitment to do God's will.

I learned this, not from reading a book, but by going through a fiery trial when I pastored in Omaha, Nebraska. My wife and I moved there and began a church from zero on May 31, 1981. Bonnie was miserable in Nebraska and longed to return to Oregon. I wanted to make her happy, but when I asked God's permission to move back I could not get a release. Most people would have moved back with or without a release from God. Perhaps the only way to ever find out if I was a blockhead or an obedient son will be to have God judge this situation. Was I hardhearted, stubborn, and insensitive to my wife? Or was I faithfully doing God's will? Only He knows. From my perspective, I desperately wanted to please both God and my wife. I felt pulled in different directions and I found it excruciatingly painful.

After several years of unsuccessfully begging for God's permission to let us move back to Oregon, I changed tactics. I reasoned that if God would not let me give Bonnie the Cascade Mountains, the Pacific Ocean, and her relatives, maybe He would let me give her a mansion on an acreage with a horse barn. I prayed, "Let me give her the best Nebraska has."

We looked at acreages for two years. I covered every single country road for a thirty-mile radius around Omaha looking for that elusive spot where we might live happily ever after. Bonnie did not want to live in Nebraska, so nothing seemed right to her. Finally, however, we did find one house she liked. It was an executive mansion on eight acres with nothing around it but cornfields. She had always said she wanted total privacy with no neighbors in sight. She liked the house and its setting.

I talked to a wealthy lady in our church and she agreed to loan me the money at 8 percent interest, two percentage points below the going rate. My calculations showed we would be able to make the payment. Excited and hopeful, I called Bonnie from church. "Bonnie, we can get that house. I found a private lender who will give us a great interest rate and we'll be able to do it."

I heard my wife saying, "I've changed my mind. You are moving too fast. I don't want that house." My last chance at happiness had melted like a snowflake in July. All the emotional pain and frustration I felt for eight years erupted like a volcano. The next thing I remember is jumping on the couch and pounding the wall as I screamed in agony. I put my fist through that wall. Then I ran out of my office and threw the door open with such force the doorknob went through that wall. I ran into the sanctuary, which was a converted school gymnasium. As loud as I could I screamed at one wall, "I hurt." Then I screamed at the other wall, "What about me?" Then I screamed my generic scream, "*Ahhhhh.*" I screamed for a solid two hours until I could not scream any more. I walked out of that building totally crushed in my spirit. A crushed spirit comes when you feel with all your heart that God has failed you. There was no more hope. God had put me in an impossible situation. He would not let me give my wife the mountains and the ocean or the mansion and the horse barn. I never wanted to pray again.

In that broken state I had to fly to Canada and preach a family camp for the Full Gospel Businessmen's Fellowship. Bonnie and I were not talking on that flight and did not sit together as we flew into Nanaimo, British Columbia. I had one day before I had to start preaching and I used it to get alone and walk on the logging trails.

I told God, "I am dead inside. I am a dead fish. These people are expecting a great camp meeting. You fed a multitude with dead fish before, so for their sake, please use me to feed them even if I am dead."

The darkness of satanic oppression was like a thick and suffocating cloud around me. Dying seemed much easier than living, if only I could die. In one last attempt to communicate with God I said, "Father, it has been eight years. I have suffered for eight years in Omaha. How long do I have to suffer?" We had been married for sixteen years, but the last eight had been lived with this terrible and constant disagreement. If God would have said, *All right, son, I will kill you,* I would have thanked Him. Suddenly God spoke clearly to me and asked, *How long did it take Noah to save his family?* I answered, "It took him about one hundred years to build the ark." God spoke again, *I want a one hundred-*

year commitment out of you to save your family.

At the absolute lowest point of my spiritual life my Father demanded my deepest commitment. I did not stop to think about it. I just said, "All right. I will give you a one hundred-year commitment to save my family." I did not see an angel come and did not even know about this principle. I did not give God that deep commitment just to get strength. I gave it to Him because He demanded it and I love Him. I never even considered saying no to Him. That first night I preached on commitment and got every man in the camp to make a one hundred-year commitment to save their families. Looking back, I am sure God did send an angel to strengthen me. When the camp meeting was over, I heard reports that people were saying it was the best camp meeting they had ever experienced.

All along God was trying to teach me to give myself to my wife. I would have given her the mountains and the ocean or a mansion and a horse barn. He taught me to say *I love you* with my time. I changed my priorities and learned to spend more time enjoying her. I began to show her my love by stopping the flow of condemning words. To communicate without condemnation is a wonderful thing. Then, one by one, He taught me how to plant miracle seeds. Those miracle seeds are encouragement, comfort, fellowship, tenderness, and compassion. (See Philippians 2:1–2.)

When I had changed enough and God had worked His plan in me, He did let us move back to the Pacific Northwest, almost nine years after that camp meeting. It has been more than seventeen years since He demanded that commitment. We now have a beautiful home in the exact place in Oregon my wife and I like the most.

Soon after I made that commitment we had our second beautiful daughter. Our oldest daughter has also given us two grandsons. Bonnie and I are getting along better than ever. The family is safe, and I only have eighty-three years left to go on my commitment.

One day in Omaha, I was doing the laundry for our family because God had taught me to use my power to help Bonnie as a way of showing her compassion. As I was taking the laundry out of the washer to put in the dryer a hot, fiery, tangible anointing came into my right hand. That was in July of 1991. The next day it went into my other hand as well, then up my arms. Then to my joy I felt it also in my feet.

Because of that anointing hundreds have been baptized in the Holy Spirit when I have laid hands on them. Many have been physically healed or set free from spiritual oppression as anointing flowed through my hands. That was one way God showed how much He loves my wife—He blessed me when I blessed her. If I had given up on my marriage I would have lost the love of my life, the unity of our family, and the anointing I delight in. Love generates spiritual power. No one can stop loving and keep spiritual power.

Another Biblical example of this principle is found in the Book of Ester. She had been selected to be queen of Persia, but no one knew she was a Jewish girl. Haman, the enemy of the Jews, had implemented a plan to exterminate the Jews on a certain day. The king had OK'd the plan and the funding to carry it out was already in the king's treasury. Ester knew that only her appeal to the king stood between the Jews and complete slaughter. She also knew that the king's policy was to kill any woman in his harem who bugged him. He could make an exception, if he chose, and stretch out a golden scepter. Then the wife would be spared.

Ester was at her lowest point when she made her deepest commitment. Literally everything was going wrong until she said, "I will go to the king, even though it is against the law.

And if I perish, I perish" (Esther 4:16). From the moment Ester made her deepest commitment to do God's will, angels were loosed on her behalf. From that moment, everything went wrong for Haman and those who hated the Jews. The tables were turned completely and the Jews gained the victory over their enemies. This true story is a great example of the principle—God gives extra strength to those who make an all-out commitment to do His will.

> For the eyes of the LORD range throughout the earth to strengthen those whose hearts are fully committed to him.
>
> —2 CHRONICLES 16:9

Chapter 6

CELEBRATE TROUBLE

*Consider it pure joy, my brothers, whenever
you face trials of many kinds, because you
know that the testing of your faith develops
perseverance. Perseverance must finish its work
so that you may be mature and complete,
not lacking anything.*
—James 1:2–4—

It is an apostolic principle of perseverance to *celebrate* trouble. Millions of Christians read these verses, but almost no one practices them. I had an unusual experience where I actually touched this principle.

When I was pastoring a church in Omaha and in the early eighties, my wife, Bonnie, and I had a series of things go wrong—four things that cost about five hundred dollars each. The diamond fell out of her ring and was lost. The air compressor on our home air conditioner stopped working, and you really need an air conditioner in the hot humid summers of Eastern Nebraska. Two other things went wrong, both of which required about five hundred dollars. When Bonnie called me to report that another big problem had developed, which would require money we did not have, I just started laughing. I said, "I have no idea how we're going to come up with an extra two thousand dollars."

Then I had an idea. These Bible verses written by the apostle James came to my mind. I said, "Let's both drive to Rax Restaurant and have a chocolate milk shake together and just celebrate all this trouble." Bonnie thought that was a great idea. She drove from home, I drove from the church, and we met at Rax. We each ordered a chocolate shake. We held hands and prayed, "Father, we do not know how to solve these problems. So we're just going to celebrate them like You said."

These problems had all come suddenly, in about one week. In 1984, two thousand dollars of extra bills seemed overwhelming to a pioneer pastor living on a small income. But miraculously, God brought in two thousand dollars from unusual sources and every need was met in thirty days. It was phenomenal. We had touched this principle, and I had a great story to tell. Later, when I traveled as an evangelist and teacher between 1997 until 2001, I told this story all over America. But I wasn't living the principle.

Finally it occurred to me that I could do better than just have one aging story to tell about this perseverance technique. I closely examined the writings of the apostle Paul where he said he had learned to delight in trials of many kinds.

> To keep me from becoming conceited because of these surpassingly great revelations, there was given me a thorn in my flesh, a messenger of Satan, to torment me. Three times I pleaded with the Lord to take it away from me. But he said to me, "My grace is sufficient for you, for my power is made perfect in weakness." Therefore I will boast all the more gladly about my weaknesses, so that Christ's power may rest on me. That is why, for Christ's sake, I delight in weaknesses,

in insults, in hardships, in persecutions, in difficulties. For when I am weak, then I am strong.

—2 CORINTHIANS 12:7–10

There are many arguments as to just what Paul's thorn in the flesh was. He said it was a messenger of Satan. To me, it seems clear that this was an evil spirit that operated in Jewish religious leaders who had rejected Christ. They followed Paul from one city to another, stirring up the Gentiles and causing riots, beatings, and imprisonments for Paul.

He was basically asking God, "Please put a big angel between me and this evil spirit and just keep it away from me." But God knew that if Paul had more trials and troubles he would stay in a greater dependence upon God. That would mean God could give him more grace and Paul would have more supernatural power.

Once Paul understood this he began to actually embrace this process. Instead of complaining about a new hardship, he would delight in it or celebrate it. Then he'd get additional power from God. If he had complained about it he would have lost the power he already had. Complaining, therefore, is one of the very worst things you can do. It has no place whatever in a life of faith. In every trial we are given a covering of grace to help us. If we praise God and react in a positive way this covering increases. If we react in a negative way this spiritual covering is lost and we face our trials in merely our own strength and wisdom. Things get much worse when we complain.

In Acts 4, we see that the early church was in a difficult situation. The very rulers who had crucified Christ had commanded the apostles not to speak or teach at all in the name of Jesus. They threatened the apostles with many things. Their reaction to this negative situation was positive. They had a powerful prayer meeting:

Now, Lord, consider their threats and enable your servants to speak your word with great boldness. Stretch our your hand to heal and perform miraculous signs and wonders through the name of your holy servant Jesus.

—ACTS 4:29–30

After they prayed, the place where they were meeting was shaken. And they were all filled with the Holy Spirit and spoke the word of God boldly.

—ACTS 4:31

All the believers were one in heart and mind. This means they were all reacting positively to this negative situation. They all wanted God to be glorified at any cost. "No one claimed that any of his possessions was his own, but they shared everything they had. With great power the apostles continued to testify to the resurrection of the Lord Jesus, *and much grace was upon them all*" (Acts 4:32–33, emphasis added).

Though the situation was difficult and life-threatening, the believers were not complaining, grumbling, expressing fear, worrying, or fretting. Instead they were praying for boldness so that they could glorify God. A covering of grace was given to the whole church because the whole church was reacting to the situation positively—in joy, boldness, praise, dependence on God, and love for one another.

Paul wrote, "The night is nearly over; the day is almost here. So let us put aside the deeds of darkness and put on the armor of light" (Rom. 13:12). God wants to cover us with grace and spiritual light. But we can lose this awesome covering of grace by negative reactions. No wonder Paul wrote to the early church, "Be joyful always; pray continually; give thanks in all circumstances, for this is God's will for you in Christ Jesus" (1 Thess. 5:16–18).

Another Biblical example would be Joseph who was sold into slavery by his brothers. Apparently his reaction to this trouble was positive because the Bible says, "The LORD was with Joseph and he prospered, and he lived in the house of his Egyptian master. When his master saw that the LORD was with him and that the LORD gave him success in everything he did, Joseph found favor in his eyes and became his attendant. Potiphar put him in charge of his household, and he entrusted to his care everything he owned" Gen. 39:2–4).

Being sold as a slave by his own brothers did not destroy Joseph with anger, bitterness, hatred, and self-pity because he reacted so positively to it God gave him even more grace. Later, Potiphar's lustful wife tried to seduce Joseph, and when he refused she accused him of trying to rape her. He was thrown into prison. Again he must have reacted positively to his negative situation because once more God was with him and gave him favor in the eyes of the prison warden who put him in charge of the whole prison.

How do we know he reacted positively? Because when he was finally exalted to the right hand of Pharaoh and his brothers appeared before him to buy food he was gracious to them. He protected and blessed them instead of getting even. God does not play favorites. He would like to be with you and me in every negative situation, giving us coverings of overcoming grace.

"All the days of the oppressed are wretched, but the cheerful heart has a continual feast" (Prov. 15:15). We could say, "All the days of those who react to their situation negatively are wretched, but those who react positively have a continual covering of grace." If we want this covering of grace we should make an all-out effort to react to negative circumstances with delight, joy, and praise like the apostles Paul and James.

This covering of grace is a covering of power that enables the believer to overcome in any kind of bad situation. It is a covering of the very presence of God. What a tragedy when we lose it by grumbling, complaining, and feeling sorry for ourselves. Then we are in the negative situations without the covering of grace. Paul writes, "Do everything without complaining or arguing, so that you may become blameless and pure, children of God without fault in a crooked and depraved generation, in which you shine like stars in the universe as you hold out the word of life" (Phil. 2:14–16).

It is like two sides of the same coin. One side says "Rejoice and celebrate your trouble." The other side says, "Never complain." Both of these spiritual techniques need a strong clarification. God wants to give us victory over problems and convert them to miracles. When I say, "What a wonderful problem this is," I am thinking of it as raw material for a miracle. By faith in Christ Jesus, I want to convert the problem into a blessing and not just leave it a problem. Also, when I am in a motel and a light is burned out I ask the management for a new light bulb. That's not complaining— that's problem solving. We need to find solutions to solve problems. Abraham had a problem when the servants of the Philistine king, Abimelech, seized one of the wells of water Abraham's servants had dug. He did not just praise God and accept this problem. The New International Version says, "Abraham complained to Abimelech." Abimelech said, "I do not know who has done this. You did not tell me, and I heard about it only today." So Abraham brought sheep and cattle and gave them to Abimelech, and the two men made a treaty. Abraham set apart seven ewe lambs from the flock, and Abimelech asked Abraham, "What is the meaning of

TWO SIDES OF THE COINAGE OF FAITH

these seven ewe lambs you have set apart by themselves?" He replied, "Accept these seven lambs from my hand as a witness that I dug this well." (See Genesis 21:25–30.)

Notice how gracious Abraham was. The word complained could be better translated, communicated. Abimelech should have been giving gifts to Abraham and apologizing. Although his men had done the wrong he never admitted to anything nor did he apologize. Abraham was the bigger person and solved the problem in a very positive way. We have to communicate and solve problems, but we must do so without being mean spirited.

We also need to learn how to *create a bubble*. I learned this many years ago when I was terribly depressed. I had been asking God to let me move from Nebraska back to Oregon. When I could not get a release to do that I asked God to let me give my wife a mansion and a horse barn—the best Nebraska had. When that option fell through with finality I felt God had forsaken me. God wanted to teach me how to give *myself* to my wife, but I did not understand His strategy.

Thick spiritual darkness was suffocating me as I walked the logging trails in Canada preparing to preach a Full Gospel Business Men's family camp meeting. Although God would not give me any of the big things I was asking for, He had blessed me with a new pair of Reebok track shoes. As I walked those trails, praying, I felt forsaken by God. But I kept thanking Him for those comfortable shoes that felt so good on my feet. When I would thank God for the shoes it felt like a bubble of spiritual oxygen came around my head. I could breathe. Over and over I thanked God for the shoes. Each time I would thank Him it was as if I was able to breathe underwater through some type of spiritual scuba gear. Not long after that God spoke to me and delivered me out of that awful despair by helping me make a deeper commitment. (See Chapter 5)

I heard about a man who was laying pipe in a ditch. When he saw the ditch was caving in on him he quickly put his hard hat over his face to create a bubble of breathable air. His coworkers dug him out immediately and the little bubble of oxygen was just enough to save his life.

Sometimes it seems that troubles are overwhelming us. We may be so weakened spiritually that converting these troubles to blessings is beyond our ability. But even in our weakest times we can find something to thank God for. As we thank Him for some small thing it creates a bubble of spiritual oxygen that keeps our faith from dying. Somehow, God will always enlighten us and empower us again if we'll just find something to praise Him for.

God uses a process to make us Christlike. If we understand this process we can cooperate with it instead of resist it. Paul understood it and cooperated with it. "For we who are alive are always being given over to death for Jesus' sake, so that his life may be revealed in our mortal body" (2 Cor. 4:11).

Imagine God looking down from heaven at two of His children. We will call them Joe and Josephine. God says to the angels, *I love my children Joe and Josephine and want total intimacy with them. I want to fill them up to all the fullness of God. But they're content with being only half full. Their situations are easy enough that they do not realize how much more of me they need and could have. So, angels, I have a strategy. I want you to back off in your protection, and I am going to let the devil bring some big trouble to them. I am hoping that when the trouble comes they'll ask Me for more grace. Then I can fill them up to fullness and give them victory. Hopefully, they'll pray the "Change me" prayer. But, angels, if they just ask Me to change the circumstance and change everyone who is bothering them—do not act on their behalf. You will mess up my plan. Do you understand?* The angels are wide-eyed and can hardly believe it. After all, they are used to giving constant protection to these "heirs of salvation." They back off, Satan moves in gleefully through this opening, and soon Joe is having all kinds of trouble. He prays, "Lord, what's going on? I was going to church, tithing, and reading my Bible. But now this goofy neighbor is having wild parties all night long. I think he's dealing drugs, too. I cannot sleep at night and he's causing the neighborhood to degenerate. I really need You to move him out. In fact, it would be real nice if You let a lightening bolt torch his house. Please, get him out of here. And Lord, my wife is going through menopause. Wow. You need to have a talk with her, Lord and teach her how to walk in the Spirit. And while You are at it, my boss is overworking me and giving promotions to his drinking buddies. Please appear to him in a dream and tell him to treat me right."

The angels are shedding big tears. They want to help Joe so badly, but God restrains them saying, *Do not move to help him. He's praying the wrong prayers.* Meanwhile Josephine is also having problems. She prays, "God, my mother-in-law is interfering so much. She's had a good life. Can't You just take her home? And my husband, Frank. Now God, how can any Christian woman live in victory when married to a man like that? Can't You rebuke him? Tell him to treat me right. He's so rude and inconsiderate. And Lord, while You are at it, would You please give us a few days of sunshine? I am so sick of this miserable rain."

The angels look to God, hoping He'll give them the "go signal" so they can help Josephine. But He says, *No. She's praying the wrong prayer.* Finally, Joe says to the Lord, "Now Father, Jesus said if I would first seek the kingdom of God and His righteousness all these things would be added to me. But I have sought you every morning for three hours and this has gone on for six months. You still haven't changed anything or anybody. I am about ready to reduce my tithe to 2 percent unless You shape up."

Then God speaks to Joe, *I cannot answer your prayers because you do not qualify. You are not seeking My righteousness first.* Joe argues, "Yes I am. You know I am seeking You three hours a day." God says, *It does not count because you are not seeking Me to change you with My righteousness. If you want to have victory you must first ask Me to change you. That's what 'Seek first My righteousness' means.* Then Joe gets it. He prays, "All right, Lord. Change me. Give me compassion for that neighbor. Help me to win him to Christ. Help me serve my boss even better, as if I am working for You. Change me so that I can treat my wife with the kind of consideration that will honor You."

God smiles and turns to the angels, *Get those buckets of grace and go pour them out on Joe. You can help him now. Give him grace to conquer and overcome all these difficulties.* Josephine finally gets it as well, and starts praying the prayer that shakes heaven, "Change me." She also is given grace to overcome. But what about you and me? Have we embraced God's process enough to cooperate with it?

Dear friend, always ask God to change you first. Celebrate trouble as raw material for miracles. Create a bubble by thanking God for some small thing you really appreciate. Become conscious of when you are complaining and stop it. Why lose your covering of grace? Praise God instead, and God's grace upon you will be increased. Be the person who never complains but rather solves problems with a good attitude.

Finally, put your troubles in perspective. They cause you to develop perseverance. The apostle James knew that perseverance, once developed would take the believer to victory, achievement, and intimacy with God so that no victory would be lacking. This is a principle of perseverance you can become skilled in.

See this principle in what the apostle Paul says. "Not only so, but we also rejoice in our sufferings, because we know that suffering produces perseverance; perseverance, character; and character, hope. And hope does not disappoint us, because God has poured out his love into our hearts by the Holy Spirit, whom he has given us" (Rom. 5:3–5).

See? He celebrated trouble, rejoicing in it, because he expected God's grace to change him by the power of the Holy Spirit. Paul wrote, "I delight in…insults" (2 Cor. 12:10). I force myself to do this. When I get good and insulted, I get angry. When I realize how angry I am, I start praising God for the insult that revealed how much hidden pride I have left. I force myself to say, "What a wonderful insult. Praise God. That was a good one. It showed me I am not as spiritual as I thought I was. Change me, Lord."

Dear friend, we all can choose to delight in weaknesses, hardships, difficulties, persecutions, and insults. These delightful things help us depend on God in our weakness—and when we are weak, then we are strong.

Chapter 7

OVERCOME EVIL
WITH GOOD

Do not be overcome by evil, but
overcome evil with good.
—Romans 12:21—

When we feel that we have been treated unjustly, we can choose to be overcome with anger, bitterness, self-pity, malice, and hatred—or we can overcome the evil with good. Many people drop out of the ministry and others drop out of church—or their marriage—because someone did something evil to them and they felt justified in quitting. If you are a little angry, you can keep going in obedience, but it is like having sand in your shoes. But when negative emotions overcome us—we quit obeying God. It is just impossible to keep cycling in success when you are stewing about injustices suffered. Most people focus on the bad things done to them, but the apostles had learned to focus on the good they could do for others.

You will either learn this technique and practice it—or eventually you will drop out of the race, angry, bitter and blaming your disobedience on the decisions of others. Any time you are feeling miserable and think it is because of the decisions of others you are in self-deception. When we are miserable it is always because of our own lack of positive decisions. Jesus taught His disciples not to focus on the bad decisions of others but to immediately make a right decision and do good—even to enemies:

> But I tell you who hear me: Love your enemies, do good to those who hate you, bless those who curse you, pray for those who mistreat you.
>
> —LUKE 6:27–28

> Do to others as you would have them do to you.
>
> —LUKE 6:31

> And if you do good to those who are good to you, what credit is that to you? Even "sinners" do that.
>
> —LUKE 6:33

> But love your enemies, do good to them…. Then your reward will be great, and you will be sons of the Most High.
>
> —LUKE 6:35

As I persevered through the church split of 1996, good things began to happen. Another church merged with us and our assets were doubled. Our bus ministry continued because a wealthy businessman who didn't even attend our church began to underwrite it.

I knew God wanted me to travel America and teach believers how to walk in love intentionally by choosing to keep their spirits sweet. Before God released me to this national ministry, He had allowed me to be severely tested. In this test, God taught me that it's possible to keep a sweet spirit even in the most extreme situations.

Another pastor took charge of our church and I began

traveling the nation holding very successful revivals. However, I kept thinking about a deacon who had teamed up with the staff member I fired. I kept feeling like God wanted me to do something more for him than I was doing.

One day I told God, "Lord, I have forgiven him, prayed for him, and blessed him. Yet I cannot get him off my mind. What more can I do?" God spoke to me, *Do good to him.* I hadn't thought of that.

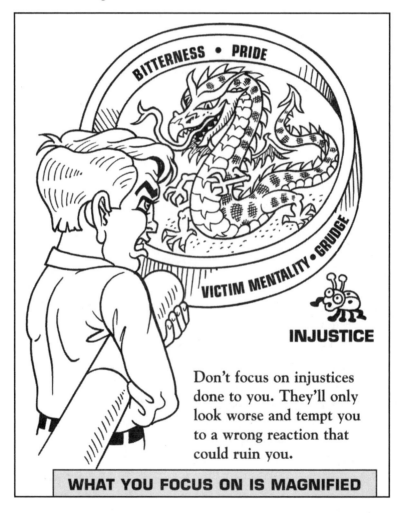

Don't focus on injustices done to you. They'll only look worse and tempt you to a wrong reaction that could ruin you.

WHAT YOU FOCUS ON IS MAGNIFIED

At that time, I was serving on the board of directors of a foundation that gave money to Christian ministries who had outreaches to children in the city of Omaha. One-tenth of their budget was spent on helping ministries to reach children all over the world. The deacon had started a worthy ministry to some of the world's poorest children in Honduras. I wrote him a letter and told him I thought I could help him get a six thousand dollar grant for his ministry if he'd fill out a grant application. He wrote a nice letter back to me and invited me to his ministry banquet. I attended that and enjoyed myself. Many people were there who had left the church in anger, but I felt God's peace and had a good time with all of them. After he received the grant, this brother called me to say he would like to have a farewell party for me before I moved away, and asked if it would be OK to invite all the people who had left the church.

We had the most wonderful farewell party. Almost all the people who had left the church were there and many gave testimonies of how they had been blessed by my ministry. The deacon testified that when I had prayed for him to be delivered from cigarettes he had seen a vision of a white horse galloping towards him. He said he thought it would kill him and it ran right through him. The spiritual impact of that knocked him to the ground and when he got up he was free from addiction to cigarettes.

I had forgotten that—but what a great thing to hear him testifying of it. So we had a really good time and I moved away with lots of reconciliation having taken place. That was my Joseph miracle. It brought good closure to that year of turmoil and trouble. But none of that would have happened if I neglected to do good for him.

If I had focused on the negative things that had been done to me, I am not sure how long I could have continued in the ministry. But by focusing on the good I could do for that brother I was helped myself. *Never* allow your focus to be on the injustices done to you. Always focus on the good you can do for others.

The principle of doing good works is great in financial matters as well. For years I have had a little saying, *"If I am going to go down, I will go down doing good."* When I pastored, if the church looked like it would go under financially I would do some new project for missions. Over and over God proved to me, that you do not go down doing good. You go back up.

> Good will come to him who is generous.
> —PSALM 112:5

Solomon wrote, "I also saw under the sun this example of wisdom that greatly impressed me" (Eccles. 9:13). Like Solomon, I heard a testimony that greatly impressed me. Although I never did retain in my memory the names of the parties involved, the principle involved went into my heart. I began practicing giving money away to other ministries when my own ministry was in trouble financially. Here's the story that taught me this important way to persevere.

A large Christian school was forced to come up with one million dollars due to new government regulations. They worked hard and came up with five hundred thousand dollars. The time limit was up and they knew they were going under as a school. The board of decision makers met and said, "Look. There's this other great Christian School somewhat smaller than ours. They only need five hundred thousand dollars. Why should the devil destroy two Christian schools? Let's give our five hundred thousand dollars to them. We'll save their school for the glory of God. We'll go down, but we'll go down doing good."

They saved that other school and a multi-millionaire

heard about it and wrote them a check for one million dollars. They did not go down doing good, they went back up.

I also heard a true story of a Chinese Christian lady who was a schoolteacher. She let her class march in a parade without the red neck scarves that were required. For that she was thrown into prison and beaten until her spirit came out of her body. She stood before Jesus and He said, "Go back to Earth. Your work is not done. Go back and do good to your enemies."

She asked permission to clean the rooms the prison guards lived in, which weren't much better than the cells. She cleaned them elaborately, polishing and scrubbing the walls and floors with a toothbrush. Other guards asked her if she would clean their rooms. Not long after she had led the guards to Christ the whole prison was converted.

When a high official came to inspect the prison he was alarmed by all the cheer and love. Prison was supposed to be a place of punishment with a lot of sad and angry faces. After an investigation, the happy state of the prison was blamed on this little Christian teacher and she was transferred to another prison.

There the same process was repeated. She was beaten until her spirit stood before Jesus. Once more He sent her back with the same words. She again did good to her enemies and another prison was totally converted. She was moved the third time and yet another prison was converted to Christ because her good deeds of love overcame the evil of atheistic hatred. After that she was martyred. She is probably one of the greatest heroines in heaven.

When your situation seems as dark as night—do good to some needy person and your light will rise in darkness. When it seems like it is the midnight of a dark time, do good and your light will become like the noonday sun. When you are sickened by your situation, do good and your healing will quickly appear. When you are going through a desert experience and life seems dry and parched, do good to someone who is worse off than you and your life will become like a well-watered garden. When you are tempted to point a finger of judgment at someone who is not doing right—stop and instead, do them good by interceding for them with a loving prayer. Stop talking maliciously and make sure your speech only benefits the listeners. Then you will ride on the heights of the land and feast on the inheritance of the Patriarchs and great men and women of faith. (See Isaiah 58:3–11.)

Focus on the good
you can do to others
— AND DO IT!

**WHAT YOU FOCUS
ON IS MAGNIFIED**

You may have been cruelly victimized, but you do not have to adopt a victim mentality—living in the smallness of mad, bad, and sad thoughts. *You* can overcome evil with good. What they did cannot destroy you. Your own response is what is most dangerous. Choosing to respond in kind, giving insult for insult and blow for blow—that can and will destroy those who indulge in it.

Sometimes in our families we get hurt most by the people we love the most. At times like that we can pout or go into isolation, ratchet up the insult war with retaliation—or—we can simply do good to them.

Once I was extremely angry at my wife, although I cannot remember why. I just remember deciding I would not sleep in the same house with her. As I angrily drove away, I decided to go to a city fifty miles away and get a motel there. Suddenly God spoke to me, *How proud do you want to be? Proud enough to get divorced? Proud enough to be out of the ministry? Proud enough to go broke financially? Proud enough to have your children backslide and be lost because their dad is a hypocrite? Proud enough to go to hell yourself? Just how far do you want to take it? How proud do you want to be?* I pulled the car over to the side of the road, stopped, hung my head, and said, "I do not want to be that proud." I turned the car around, went home, and mowed the lawn.

Dear friend, I wasn't in the best of moods when I returned home. But just by starting to do good, my ugly mood was affected for the better. From that experience I learned that if I was angry I could help myself and the whole family by using my energy to do something good. You do not have to be in a good mood to do something good. You do not have to feel good to do something good. You do not have to be thinking good thoughts to do something good. Just do good and soon your mood, your feelings, and your thoughts will be greatly improved. That will improve your health, your relationships, your finances and most of all your relationship with God.

I learned that doing good helps to *keep* us in a good mood. I do not wait until I am in a bad mood to help with the dishes or clean my wife's car. If I habitually do kind deeds at home and wherever I am, I find that I am almost always in a good mood and am blessed with good thoughts. Doing good is a great way to feel good—about life and about yourself. One of my favorite sayings is, "It feels good to be good." So why wait? If you are sick of feeling bad—begin doing good things for others immediately—*now*.

Look again at the words of Jesus. "But love your enemies, do good to them, and lend to them without expecting to get anything back. Then your reward will be great, and you will be sons of the Most High, because he is kind to the ungrateful and wicked. Be merciful, just as your Father is merciful" (Luke 6:35–36).

By doing good to our enemies we become mature, Christlike Christians—full-grown adult sons of God. We are already sons of God, if we've been born of the Spirit. However, we can be most infantile in our behavior and thoughts. Doing good to those who are doing bad to us keeps us from being overcome by evil. It also causes us to be greatly rewarded in all kinds of ways, but first among them would be increased intimacy with God.

When we do good to those we are angry at we overcome, first of all, the evil within ourselves. Our good deeds may overcome their evil as well, as in the case with the Chinese teacher. But even if they do not change—our good deeds change us and we are rewarded with a deeper intimacy with God. We'll hear God's voice more easily and be heard by Him in prayer without hindrance. We'll grow up in Christ. We will not quit obeying God and justify it with some puny excuse about who was mean to us. We'll have the kind of perseverance that causes us to be "mature and complete, not lacking anything" (James 1:4).

Chapter 8
ARMOR UP

*Put on the full armor of God so that you can
take your stand against the devil's schemes.*
—Ephesians 6:11—

O ur ability to persevere in obedience until great achievements are accomplished is in direct proportion to the
amount of spiritual armor we wear. Most Christians are
almost naked when it comes to this armor. A few know how
to quote verses that speak of God's armor, but even those folks
usually do not know how to actually put it on.

I often hear Christians boastfully singing about how they
will go to the enemy's camp and plunder it. Perhaps they
think Satan's camp will be deserted and they can tiptoe in
like little naked fairies, grab something from Satan's treasures
and boogie out of there. Woe to them if the enemy happens
to be *in* his camp.

I met one woman who claimed to put the armor of God
on every day. She did a daily ritual of reciting Bible verses
about God's armor and declared she was putting it on. "Now I
put on the helmet of salvation. Now I put on the belt of truth.
Now I put on the breastplate of righteousness. Now I put on
the boots of spiritual readiness. Now I pick up the shield of
faith, and now I take the sword of the Spirit." I thought to

myself, *Lady, you might as well be trusting in a lucky rabbit's foot.* What she was doing was nothing more than superstition dressed up like faith.

It does not take long to describe how to *really* put on the armor of God. You put on the belt of truth when you *turn at the correction* of the Word of God. Then you are not walking in self-deception. You put on the breastplate of righteousness when you *do* what the Word of God says to do. You put on the helmet of salvation when you *meditate* on the Word of God. Then your mind is guarded. When the devil rings in on your mental line, all he gets is a busy signal.

You pick up the shield of faith when you *believe* what the Word of God says. You put on the spiritual boots of readiness when you *memorize* the Word of God. You are ready for anything when you have a true love relationship with God's Word and the author of the Word, the Holy Spirit that vibrates in it. You truly are wielding the Sword of the Spirit when you *speak* the Word of God under the unction of the Holy Spirit. If your mouth is full of complaining—then the Sword of the Spirit is not in your mouth.

The seventh piece of the armor is to "*pray in the Spirit* on all occasions with all kinds of prayers" (Eph. 6:18, emphasis added). Live in a love relationship with the Word of God and the Spirit of God and you will be fully armored. This is no ordinary armor. It is God's armor. Imagine yourself dressed up in a suit of armor belonging to some famous knight. As far as anyone would know, it would not be you inside that armor—it would be the warrior knight. In the same way, when you are dressed in God's armor you really scare the enemy because, when dressed in God's armor, God's power and presence is all around you. The enemy does not just see you anymore. He sees the God who is protecting you.

It takes time and effort to be fully armored up, and there

are no shortcuts. Seek to know and please God by reading His Word, meditating on it, believing it, doing it, memorizing it, and speaking it. Then pray in the Holy Spirit. Remember, the Holy Spirit is the greatest "search engine" in all of creation. He can search what no computer can search—the mind and heart of God. Knowing a few verses is not enough. You must truly have a love relationship with the Word and Spirit of God.

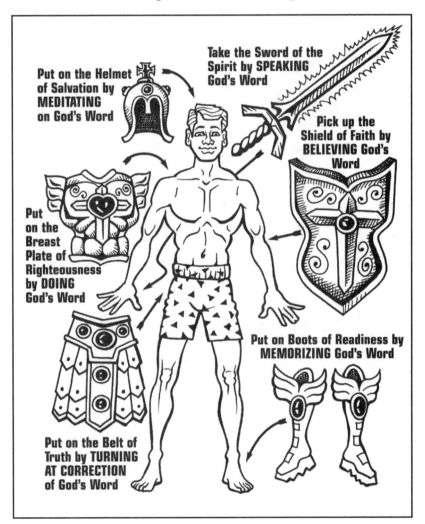

Once, as a young pastor, I counseled a couple regarding their marriage problems. I told the man that he was part of the problem, and showed him what he needed to work on, and I did the same with his wife. The next Sunday, just before I was going to preach, that lady came up to me and declared, "I have a Word from God for you. I had a vision, and I saw a wrecking ball hitting this church and destroying it. God told me He is going to destroy this church because you are a bribe taker."

The lady was such a whacko that she thought her husband had financially bribed me to say that even part of their problem was her problem. I knew her word was false, but that event shocked me. I wondered how I could stand the emotional trauma of ministry if people were going to treat a nice guy like me in this way. I was young and inexperienced in just how deceived some people are, so her opinion of me mattered a lot more than it should have. The mature apostle Paul said, "I care very little if I am judged by you or by any human court" (1 Cor. 4:3). If we are all shook up when people misjudge us, it is a sign of our own immaturity.

The next day I cancelled all my appointments. I cancelled the following day's appointments as well and for those two days I did nothing but read the Bible. I was looking for verses to give me strength and hope so that I could survive in the ministry instead of withering under the verbal bombardment of judgmental people who had planks in their own eyes.

I found verses that gave me hope and typed them out. Then I cut them out in small strips and taped them to my phone, my wall, my door, my typewriter and any other place in my office where my eyes would easily see them. Then I went on in ministry, with the helmet of salvation back on my head, new boots on my feet, and a new sharp sword in my mouth. My shield of faith was freshly polished.

The devil that spoke through that deceived woman found

my armor a little thin. I had to armor up *after* I got hit hard and nearly dropped out of the ministry. The idea is to be continually armoring up so that when the day of evil comes you do not have to cancel your appointments and get alone with the Word of God. You and I should be ready when the attack comes. The only way to be ready is to get into God's Word every day and practice it continually.

We need to develop such a love for God's Word that it is not a chore to read it, memorize it, or study it. Practicing it should become our delight. *Our love is shown for God's Word when we set out to do it.* For instance, God's Word teaches, "Do to others what you would have them do to you" (Matt. 7:12).

The Bible says, "Do not let any unwholesome talk come out of your mouths, but only what is helpful for building others up according to their needs, that it may benefit those who listen" (Eph. 4:29). I have memorized that verse so that it is another layer of protection on my boots. It is part of my belt—because I have turned at its correction. It is part of my helmet, because I often meditate about how to communicate without speaking condemnation. It is part of my sword, because I often quote it.

Here is what I do to have a great relationship with God's Word. First, I listen to it on CD while I drive. I do this over and over, going through the Bible at least three times a year just while driving. I also study God's Word for sermon preparation. Nothing gets you into God's Word like having to study in order to teach some class. Why not become a teacher of some Bible class so you have to study in order to feed others? Why not become a spiritual mentor to some new convert or young person? They will ask you questions you cannot answer and then you will have to study. I also read or quote at least one chapter of the Bible each day.

When I was a boy, I collected fossils and bird feathers. Now I collect "just like Jesus" verses, "sweet spirit verses," and "Jesus is God" verses. Pastor Don Cox listened to one of my sermons and corrected me afterwards. He said that when I preach a salvation sermon I should always quote words from Jesus and particularly verses where Jesus spoke about hell. So I started memorizing verses where Jesus spoke about hell and including those in my salvation sermons. The results are wonderful. I win far more people to Christ as a result of collecting and using those verses. My sword has an even sharper point (convicting power) than before.

Another thing I do is to think deeply about what I am hearing or studying or about some Bible verse, story, or principle. I ponder it and go over it in my mind. Like a cow ruminating on what she's already eaten, I chew the cud so to speak. I mentally chew on what I have already put into my system. I ask God questions as to what something means—or why He put it in the Bible. Notice—if you put a lot in by listening to it—you will have a lot to ruminate on. Know what the Bible says. Then think about what it means and how to apply it while you go through your day. Most of all, I believe the Bible. I believe the words of Jesus. I believe the Bible is inspired by the Holy Spirit. That belief is my shield against doubt, worry, and fear.

None of this is hard to do. But if you play computer games by the hour, or read novels or newspapers by the hour, it is not likely you will have much armor. Instead of devoting yourself to God's Word, you may be devoting yourself to something that cannot possibly protect you in spiritual battles. Innocent things that are not sinful can be used of Satan to distract us from what is more helpful and needed. Those who say, "I just do not have time for reading the Bible," are *really* saying, "I haven't made Bible-reading a priority—because I do take time to do a lot of things that are not as important."

In World War II, the Nazi's built a state-of-the-art battleship called the *Bismarck*. It was heavily armor-plated. Two older British battleships attacked the *Bismarck*. Their shells hit the target—but just bounced off. One gunner on the *Bismarck* fired a salvo at the HMS *Hood* and the shell pierced the ship's armor. The shell exploded in the magazine of the ship and the bigger explosion that resulted blew the ship in half. It sank instantly and two thousand brave British sailors died. The other British ship retreated. If you are lightly armored, a retreat is your best strategy to stay alive. But use your retreat to armor up, and do not make retreat a permanent thing.

Many Christians bravely attack the enemy but they rush into battle with little armor and like the men on the HMS *Hood*—they get slaughtered. The Word of God will keep you if you keep on loving it. Do not wait until the day of evil comes. Put your armor on now—before you need it.

Here is an exercise that will immediately improve your armor. "You come to the help of those who gladly do right, who remember your ways" (Isa. 64:5). Now, "muttertate" (meditate) on that idea. Say that over and over to yourself. Now say, "I gladly do right. I remember God's ways. He's coming to my help. Praise God." You just picked up the shield of faith by believing the Word. You put on the helmet of salvation by meditating on the Word. You put on the boots of readiness by memorizing that simple verse. The sword of the Spirit was in your mouth when you quoted it. If you have not been gladly doing what is right, but rather grudgingly doing what is right, then turn at the correction of the Word and you will have the belt of truth firmly in place. Go forth today gladly doing what is right and remembering God's ways and you will be wearing the breastplate of righteousness.

Once, when deeply moved in worship, I asked God to

teach me how to love Him the way He wanted to be loved. His first response to me was, *Love me like Mary who sat at my feet.* Mary sat and listened to Christ's teaching, His Word. The very first way God wanted me to show Him love was to show love for His Word. Then He said, *Love Me like John who leaned on My breast. Love Me like the good Samaritan. Love Me like the women who anointed my feet. Love Me like Abraham who always obeyed me.*

Get alone with God in prayer and you will love Him like John did—who put his ear over Christ's heart. Help hurting and suffering people and He will count it as if you did it for Him. *Spiritual leaders are the "feet" of the body of Christ,* God explained to me. They carry the weight of the body (responsibility) and they take the most abuse. That is why I do all I can to strengthen and refresh pastors and spiritual leaders. It is a special way to show love to Christ and wash His feet. Finally, obedience says it all. If we love God we will obey Him. I urge you to show love to God today by getting into His Word and asking the Holy Spirit to teach you new applications. Then, when the battle rages, you will be able to persevere unto victory for the glory of God.

One last point. So many have quit obeying and are no longer fulfilling the call of God. The circumstances were too difficult. The people they had to work with were too mean. Listen, of course the circumstances will be difficult and certain people will be vicious. But that is never the real reason people drop out. *The real reason people quit obeying is always found in themselves—not in others.* They quit because they were lightly armored.

Lightly-armored people should retreat—but not quit. After getting away from the heat of the battle, they should armor up and then fulfill their calling. Are you going to quit and then just offer God an excuse? I warn you, He does not tolerate excuses. If you think He will accept an excuse for why you quit obeying—you need to wake up from your spiritual deception. Jesus said, "Not everyone who says to me, 'Lord, Lord,' will enter the kingdom of heaven, but only he who does the will of my Father who is in heaven" (Matt. 7:21). Retreat if you must, and rest. Then armor up and obey.

> Now I commit you to God and the word of his grace, which can build you up and give you an inheritance among all those who are sanctified.
>
> —ACTS 20:32

Many believers have so little armor they are like little naked fairies. Their only hope is that Satan won't be in his camp when they come to plunder it.

Chapter 9
CHANGE THE EQUATION OF WEARINESS

*Let us not become weary in doing good,
for at the proper time we will reap a harvest
if we do not give up.*
—Galatians 6:9—

Giving up is always a choice. Giving up is never something we *have* to do if it seems we have no other options. If you think you have no choice in this matter, you are deceived. "But I don't control the circumstances," you might say. True. But whether you give up or not is totally within the power of your choice. To understand this concept of choosing not to give up you must understand what I call The Equation of Weariness. Here it is:

> When all I know to do + my very best effort + a very
> long time = not enough.

If you are living in this equation, it means that chronic weariness is trying to strangle your spiritual life. The devil will be quick to come around and sympathize with you. In mock compassion he will say, "Oh, you've done all you know how to do. My, my. You've given it your *very* best effort. It has been a long, long, long time. But look. It is still not enough. Oh, dear. Let's go over that again. You've done all you know how to do, and you gave it your very best effort. And it has been a long, long, long time. But, it just isn't enough. You know, there isn't another option. You'll have to give up."

The devil will go over this equation not just twice or three times, but hundreds of times until you are practically punch drunk, and in a daze of discouragement and hopelessness. Some people are like the boxer who got hung up in the ropes of the ring while the opponent reined blow after blow to his head. Each time the devil says "You've done all you know how to do," it is yet another blow to the head. "You gave it your best effort"—another blow. "It has been a long, long, long time"—one more blow. But the knockout punch is always, "But, look. It is just not enough. There's nothing else you can do. Quitting is your only option. God will understand."

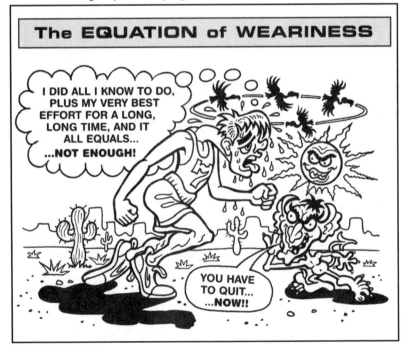

108

Remember, there are no excuses that justify a cessation of obedience. Try saying something stupid to God such as, "But I did all I knew how to do." No—do not try saying that. It will not be accepted. "But Father," you may ask, "what else can I do but quit?" Your Father will say, *My child, we do not quit. We just change the equation. You see, you really do not know very much, after all. You've got to inject more knowledge into that side of the equation. Your best effort is not enough. You need to network with others and get them praying for and with you. As you wait on Me in prayer I will increase your power. Then, give Me total commitment and you will have a victory—no exceptions.*

Spiritual leaders must be constantly changing this equation. That is one reason why we must read good books. We have to keep learning. The pastor who quits learning is going to be a weary man real soon. It is impossible to lead a vibrantly growing church if you yourself are not growing. The best book to read and study is, of course, the Bible. I read other books as well to find additional illustrations for Biblical principles. God may show someone else an insight I would never see on my own.

Many people are weary in their marriages, yet they never buy a marriage book or attend a seminar on marriage healing. They think they have done all they know how to do—but it is not very much. Others are weary with health problems. But they have not gone to a health food store and purchased one of the many outstanding books on how to maintain or regain health. Still others are exhausted in their personal struggle against financial problems. They wonder if they should just give up and go bankrupt, even though there is a huge selection of wonderful books on how to make, manage, save, and invest finances. God beckons to all, "Come listen to My wisdom."

The heart of the discerning acquires knowledge; the ears of the wise seek it out.

—Proverbs 18:15

By wisdom a house is built, and through understanding it is established; through knowledge its rooms are filled with rare and beautiful treasures.

—Proverbs 24:3–4

Ask the Holy Spirit to lead you into all truth and to teach you all things. He's the greatest Teacher of all. He will lead you to resources that will give you the knowledge you need. He will protect you from error as you read, helping you "eat the meat and leave the bones."

Many people are struggling alone in their own power trying to solve their problems. They need help—but they do not ask for it or seek it out. Perhaps it is pride or false humility to think they should not bother anyone with their problems. The Bible teaches, "Bear ye one another's burdens, and so fulfill the law of Christ" (Gal. 6:2, KJV). If your power is not sufficient, you must recruit more power by finding and recruiting prayer partners. The spiritual leader who wants to avoid weariness should constantly be building a network of friends, wise counsel, and advisors. We are in this thing together.

Power can be increased by prayer. Dr. Bernard Johnson told me personally, "Much prayer, much power. Little prayer, little power." He was known as the "Billy Graham of Brazil," and led nearly three million people to Christ in great stadium crusades in his lifetime. Hundreds of thousands were miraculously healed, delivered from demonic oppression, and baptized in the Holy Spirit in his ministry. He did not give up because he was constantly changing the equation of weariness by waiting on God in prayer.

The apostle Paul faced so many obstacles he could have become weary in doing good, but he chose instead to change the power part of the equation. His advice to spiritual leaders and laymen alike is, "Pray continually" (1 Thess. 5:17). If you pray continually, you are continually changing that equation by adding more power.

Those who only change the equation when they become weary are playing Russian roulette with their ministries. Sooner or later, they will quit and give God an excuse for why they just could not continue. It is important to avoid weariness in the first place. That is done by continually giving attention to the left side of that equation. The leaders who discipline themselves to continually learn, network, and pray are constantly growing in knowledge, resources, and spiritual power.

I do not remember where I read this quote, but it went like this, "If the devil cannot make you sin, he'll make you busy." How true. If you are too busy to read, network, and pray, you soon will have a crisis of weariness. If you blame

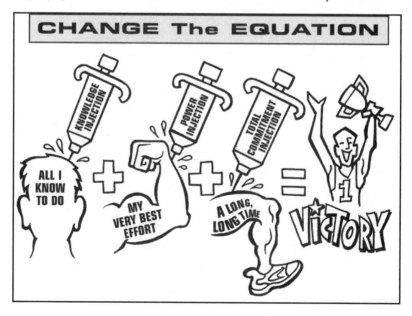

the weariness on the crisis at hand, you will move into self-deception. The reason we get overcome with weariness can never be blamed on someone else or some circumstance. We are only overcome by weariness when we choose to be.

We should work hard for the Lord and use up our strength serving Him. It is a good thing to work so hard for God that we feel exhausted. I love to serve God with all my might. We do not want to take it so easy that we never become tired. Rather, we should give our 100 percent effort daily, using all we know and all our power to please God. That necessitates daily renewal. I do not avoid weariness by means of laziness. I avoid chronic weariness by daily renewal:

> He gives strength to the weary and increases the power of the weak. Even youths grow tired and weary, and young men stumble and fall; but those who hope in the LORD will renew their strength. They will soar on wings like eagles; they will run and not grow weary, they will walk and not be faint.
>
> —ISAIAH 40:29–31

Use up your strength serving God. Give it your all. When that is used up, renew your strength rather than quitting. That is where your choosing comes in. You must choose to renew your strength instead of choosing to quit. Natural strength—physical, mental, and emotional—will be used up in God's service, and it will get used up quickly. Even those with the most natural strength and stubborn determination will drop out. Only those who continually renew their strength by depending on God, seeking God, and hearing from God will keep obeying to victory and great achievements. You can stumble and fall, or you can mount up on eagles wings. It is your choice.

Chapter 10

ENCOURAGE
SOMEONE ELSE

*But encourage one another daily, as long as
it is called Today, so that none of you may be
hardened by sin's deceitfulness.*
—Hebrews 3:13—

Encouraging someone else keeps *you* from becoming hardened by sin's deceitfulness. I do not encourage others just for their benefit. If encouragement comes out of my mouth I will be the first person who is blessed. My listener will be the second. "Therefore encourage one another and build each other up, just as in fact you are doing" (1 Thess. 5:11).

The apostle Paul was always thinking of who he could encourage and how he could best accomplish that. As a result of this mind-set and heart attitude he was always encouraged because encouragement sought him out.

"He who refreshes others will himself be refreshed" (Prov. 11:25). This is a spiritual law. When you encourage someone else you are putting a target on your own back. You become a man or woman marked for encouragement. Angels, armed with arrows of encouragement will see that target on you—and shoot you full of encouragement.

The encourager is targeted for encouragement.

It feels GREAT to be encouraged by God!

I have been shot with many verbal arrows of discouragement. I had to learn to lift up the shield of faith and let those arrows stick in my shield. But when an angelic arrow of encouragement goes into my back, I gain new strength. Instead of slumping over in pain I jump up with new enthusiasm and power.

Many days I desperately need to be encouraged. Without encouragement I could not continue to do God's will and be a fruitful minister of the gospel. So to make sure I have a continual source of encouragement being shot into me I seek to encourage others daily. Give encouragement and it will be given to you—in abundance. Jesus said, "Give and it will be given to you. A good measure, pressed down, shaken together and running over, will be poured into your lap. For with the measure you use, it will be measured to you" (Luke 7:38).

We often think this refers only to money. While it *can* apply to money it *especially* applies to encouragement. We achieve in direct proportion to our courage. If we encourage others, we'll be given lots of courage. Therefore, the one who wants to achieve the most for God should set out to be a master of encouragement.

One day I inquired of the Lord, "What will you consider my greatest achievement?" I thought of the thousands of bus kids I had enlisted to ride church buses. I thought of the bus ministries I had started in fourteen western states when I first traveled as an evangelist. I thought of the church I had founded and all we'd given to missions. I thought of the soul-winning booklet I had written that had been translated into many languages with more than two hundred fifty thousand copies in print. I thought of the radio ministry in our local area and also the stations I had been on in England and South Africa.

God surprised me. Instead of picking from those achievements He beamed into my heart this thought, "Your greatest achievement will probably be someone you encourage who will go forth and do even greater things than you have done."

I keep those words constantly in mind. I never know who that person will be—so I set out to encourage everyone—as much as I can. When little children come to my services I like to greet them and tell them how important they are. I like to preach directly to them. Who knows? Encouraging one child to go on with God may be my greatest achievement.

When I speak to teenagers I am always aware that one of them might go forth to accomplish more for God than I have. Perhaps it will be some woman or girl. It could be encouraging some elderly person to give himself or herself to intercession. After all, intercession is the highest of all ministries and the elderly have more time for it and often more character—developed over a lifetime. If I can encourage one of them to realize their importance perhaps their prayers will influence the course of nations.

Remember the story of Jonathan and David? Jonathan and his armor bearer attacked the Philistine outpost, scaling a cliff to get to the enemy. Saul and Jonathan were the only ones in the whole army that even had swords. The other troops were trembling with fear and many were deserting to hide in holes and caves. Yet when Jonathan topped that cliff the power of God hit the enemy soldiers and they fell before Jonathan. Then God sent an earthquake and a panic so that the whole Philistine army was thrown into confusion and started killing each other. (See 1 Samuel 14.)

That was a tremendous victory. Yet it was not Jonathan's greatest achievement. His greatest achievement was when he took off his royal robe, tunic, bow, and belt and gave them to David. (See 1 Samuel 18:4.) He encouraged David and said that though he, Jonathan, was heir to King Saul's throne he knew God was going to make David the king. Jonathan pledged to be his right hand man. What an encourager. David went on to do even greater exploits than Jonathan.

Jonathan's greatest achievement —
encouraging David.
What's your greatest achievement?
Who will you encourage?

Stop and think. Does it take more spirituality to kill a
Philistine or to give up your kingdom for another?

Give up trying to promote yourself so that you are
viewed as "the greatest" by others. Instead, view each one you
minister to as perhaps "the one" who with the help of your
encouragement will do even greater achievements than you.

The apostle Barnabas preached great sermons and had a miracle ministry with mighty signs and wonders. But his greatest achievement was his encouragement to Saul of Tarsus. Saul (Paul) went on to write thirteen books of the Bible. Barnabas wrote none. Yet his encouragement was a major factor in Paul's great achievements.

As you consider how to be a master of encouragement— remember we can encourage through words, financial gifts, personal visits and many other ways. My dad was most encouraged when I took time to write a letter to him thanking him for many things I hadn't thanked him for when I was living at home. I mentioned the two horses he'd given me and the yearly 4-H calves, which I sold to provide for a college fund. He wrote me back to say that getting my letter was the most meaningful thing that had ever happened to him. He had lain awake all night too emotionally stirred to sleep. After his death I was helping Mom clean out his dresser and I found my letter, saved all those years as one of his greatest treasures.

An elderly pastor friend confided in me how devastated he was. His granddaughter had been suffering from grand mal epileptic seizures. To protect her, he moved her from her apartment into his own home. One day she was running water to take a bath. When the water kept running a long time he broke open the door. She had knelt by the bathtub to wash her hair and suffered a seizure while kneeling there. When he opened the door—there was his precious granddaughter drowned to death—in his own house in spite of all his efforts to protect her. Imagine his pain.

I knew that words can be either powerful or meaningless so I prayed that God would help me say something encouraging to this dear man. I sent him a note saying that many people live long lives but never feel loved. Although his granddaughter did not live a long life, her life was meaningful because she knew how much she was loved by her grandfather. The way I said this seemed especially articulate, as if the Holy Spirit was inspiring my words. Later when I saw him in person he hugged me and said my note had been a major source of comfort and encouragement to him.

There are a few verses from Song of Solomon that create a mental picture of what I want my life to be for the glory of God. "You are a garden locked up, my sister, my bride; you are a spring enclosed, a sealed fountain. Your plants are an orchard of pomegranates with choice fruits, with henna and nard, nard and saffron, calamus and cinnamon, with every kind of incense tree, with myrrh and aloes and all the finest spices. You are a garden fountain, a well of flowing water streaming down from Lebanon" (Song of Sol. 4:12–15).

I want my life to be like a beautiful garden for God. Each achievement is like some kind of a flower, bush, or tree. My big achievements would be like fruit-bearing trees. Lesser achievements would be like bushes. Little deeds of kindness would be like individual flowers—small but fragrant. We are all creating the garden that we'll present to Christ. Each encouraging word and deed will live on in God's sight as something beautiful.

In my mind, building a church would be a "tree" in my garden while encouraging someone would be a small but fragrant flower. However, when I get to heaven, God may view something like building a church as a small flower while my "trees"—my biggest achievements—may be when I took a little extra time out of a busy schedule to encourage someone's heart.

My goal in life is to bring God massive glory. That's my constant prayer. When I think about what I have been able to do for God there is a huge gap between what I want to do for

Him and what I have done. My love for Him is so great that one lifetime could not express what I feel. Although I would like to bring Him massive glory through my one life in my one lifetime—I often think that my influence will have to be trans-generational in order to bring God the kind of glory that I desire to give Him.

Andy Andrews, in one of his books, talked about a Person of the Week award awarded by *ABC News* to a man named Norman Borlag. They said he was responsible for saving the lives of three billion people. He was a scientist—a botanist—who developed corn and wheat varieties that could grow in very arid places—thus preventing famine deaths of multiplied millions.

Andy Andrews pointed out that the award should have been given to the man who encouraged Norman Borlag. Henry Wallace was Vice President under President Roosevelt and had a vision for helping mankind through the science of botany. He got the funding for a laboratory in Mexico and personally recruited Norman Borlag to run it.

Then Andrews paused to consider that perhaps the award should have gone to George Washington Carver. The famous black botanist had taken an interest in Henry Wallace when Wallace was just a little boy. Mr. Carver inspired young Wallace with a vision to help humanity through botany. Carver himself had changed the South when God showed him the secrets within the peanut. He would often take young Henry by the hand out into the fields where he taught him the scientific names for plants. Surely it was his encouragement that put the vision in Henry Wallace to save millions of lives through botany.

Then Andrews made one more consideration. Perhaps the award should be given to farmer Carver. He was a slave owner during the Civil War but treated his slaves as family. Some terrorist desperadoes kidnapped several of his slaves and murdered one of them, a young mother. Farmer Carver risked his life to trade a horse to the terrorists for that unfortunate lady's little baby. Then he adopted the child as his own so that his name from then on was not George Washington, but George Washington Carver.

Farmer Carver did not know that when he adopted that little black baby his kind deed would result in physical salvation for three billion people several generations later. Do you see why the encouragers will be getting some of the biggest rewards in heaven?

Live in such a way that encouragement is always seeking you out. Make sure a big target is on your back for those angels of encouragement to see. Let your prayer be, "Lord, make me a master of encouragement." The kind of achievements and victories that will have an eternal significance will always be in direct proportion to your encouragement of others. Who can you encourage today?

Chapter 11

SEE THROUGH IT
TO A VISION

*Let us fix our eyes on Jesus, the author and
perfecter of our faith, who for the joy set
before him endured the cross, scorning its
shame, and sat down at the right hand of the
throne of God. Consider him who endured such
opposition from sinful men, so that you will not
grow weary and lose heart.*
—Hebrews 12:2–3—

Notice that Jesus endured the cross because he saw through the crucifixion experience to a vision of a redeemed church from every tribe and tongue. He was able to get through it because He was going to it. He had a vision, a dream. To get to the fulfillment of His vision, He was willing to go through the horrible things He endured.

I was pastoring in Omaha, Nebraska, when I finally understood this principle. One day God spoke to me, *Are you leading to—or just getting through?* I answered, "Lord, I am just trying to get through another day." Then the Holy Spirit let me know that if I was not leading the church *to* anything, I wasn't being a leader. He also showed me that by not having a clear vision of what I was going *to,* my ability to get *through* the present difficulties was hindered.

Imagine that you must cross a swamp in the dark of night. If there was a light on the other side of the swamp, you could head straight across it and press on because you would be going to the light. But, suppose there was no light on the other side, and you really did not know which way to go? You might wander around in that swamp until the alligators got you.

Dreams and visions energize us. We can get through the greatest of difficulties if we are concentrating on getting to a Holy Spirit-inspired dream. So what is your dream? What is your vision? Many would say, "I really don't have one. I'm too busy just trying to get through my problems." If that is what you say, I can tell you something about yourself: you really are not getting through your swamp. You are stuck, bogged down in it. Every day is much the same: the same bugs bite you, day after day, because you are not going through the swamp. You just live there—and you are dying there. "Where there is no vision, the people perish" (Prov. 29:18, KJV).

Dream again. This is the process of hope. Hope sees the vision. Faith takes you to the vision. Hope is like the guidance system of a rocket, locking onto a target. Faith is the rocket engine that takes you to the target. Faith and hope work together, but faith has nothing to work with if you do not dream, or if you have no vision. "Now faith is the substance of things hoped for, the evidence of things not seen" (Heb. 11:1, KJV). Faith gives substance to things you hope for. Faith brings the dream into reality.

God loves to help people achieve a worthy dream or vision. The devil may oppose it, but who can be against us when God is for us? When the greater One is helping us, all things are possible. But we must first desire it and imagine it. If our hearts are loyal to God, our desires will be those that glorify God.

123

Don Cox taught me years ago, "God gets praise for who He is. He gets glory for what He does. It brings God glory to grant your desire. God wants to give you the desire of your heart so He can get glory for His name." You see, it is the glory of a good parent to bless his or her child. It is the glory of God to bless His children.

One of my favorite Bible verses is Jeremiah 32:40–41. "I will make an everlasting covenant with them: I will never stop doing good to them, and I will inspire them to fear me, so that they will never turn away from me. I will rejoice in doing them good." If you have made Jesus Christ your Lord, then you are in this everlasting covenant and God promises you that He will never stop doing good to you. In fact, that is how God gets His pleasure. He rejoices in doing good to His people—in helping them achieve godly dreams and visions. He gets no pleasure from judging the wicked, although it is something He has to do.

Do not let doubt and unbelief rob you of your rightful dream. God will help you. God taught me that He had preplaced possibilities all around me. He showed me that He had redeemed me to give me Christ's infinite possibilities. Zacchaeus was too short to see Jesus as people crowded around Him. But God had made sure someone planted a sycamore tree near the road some forty years earlier so that a mature branch would be right there when Zacchaeus needed to climb out on it in order to see Jesus. (See Luke 19:2–8.)

David wanted to conquer Jerusalem, but that great walled city had defied Israel for hundreds of years. They taunted David, "Even the blind and the lame can tip over your assault ladders." Because David dared to dream of conquering that city God showed Him the pre-placed possibility—the water shaft. It had been there all along, but the doubters never realized it was the key to conquering the city. David's men crawled through it and captured Jerusalem, making it his capital. (See 2 Samuel 5:8.)

In the days of the Judges, the Canaanite armies were too difficult for Israel to conquer. The men said, "We cannot defeat them. They have nine hundred iron chariots. If we line up for battle they'll just run over us with those heavy war wagons. We cannot stand against them."

It took a woman named Deborah to find the preplaced possibility of God. She must have prayed, "Lord, all things are possible with you. Surely you have a way for us to conquer these wicked people who oppress us." God told her that He would lure Sisera to the Kishon River Valley. It was so easy for God. On the day of the battle He made a flash flood that turned the river valley into a quagmire. The heavy iron chariots sank into the mud and became a liability. Israel won a great victory. But notice—the river valley was there all along—pre-placed, just waiting for some man or woman of faith to discover it. (See Judges 4–5.)

I had wanted to record another music album for thirty years, but could not figure out how to finance it. It seemed to me I would need about ten thousand dollars to do it, and where that money would come from was beyond me. Then the Holy Spirit taught me that my possibilities are already in place, waiting for me to discover them. That opened my eyes.

I was holding a meeting in Evansville, Indiana, and sang a song I had written. Someone had loaned me a guitar and the pastor accompanied me on the keyboard. He played just like a studio musician and when we went out to eat after the service, I asked him, "Have you ever recorded albums?" He told me he helped many people make albums and that he had his own recording studio in his church.

Instantly I knew this man was my preplaced possibility. I said, "Would you record an album with me?" He said, "For you, I will do it for one hundred dollars a song." That was a price I could work with. Over the next few months, I recorded one song at a time. I would send one to him, he arranged it and recorded a musical background. I paid for one song at a time and finally flew to Indiana and recorded the voice tracks. Now I joyfully sing my songs with professional background music as I travel America.

Once while working on a sermon God beamed a thought into my spirit and I typed out what I received immediately. Then I stared at what I had typed and knew God had spoken it to me. It was a stunning truth. This is what I typed, "The inability to break a large dream down into small measurable first-down type goals is a greater hindrance to success than the devil himself."

Many people have a dream—but they are not moving ahead toward it. They never take the first step—so it is of no effect in giving them courage to get through present difficulties. They are not really "going to it," because they do not know how to break it down into small, measurable objectives. When God taught me this, I immediately put the truth to work. That was when I started doing one song at a time with my friend, Greg Hitchcock. Each song I sent to him, and each arrangement I paid for, was like a measurable goal. In football language, each completed song was like a first down. When the album was finished, it was a "touchdown," so to speak.

As I travel I meet people who have a dream of writing a book. I share this truth with them because unless they start writing a little bit each day, they will never achieve their dream. Imagine a coach talking to a football team. "What's your dream, boys? What's your vision?" One player says, "Coach, we want to become a legend. We want to be the team that wins more Super Bowls than any team in history."

"That's a wonderful dream, men. But we'll need to break that down in order to achieve it. What would we have to do first before we become a legend?"

"We'd have to win our first Super Bowl."

"Right. Keep breaking it down. What would we have to do before we win our first Super Bowl?"

"We'd have to win our league championship so we could play in the Super Bowl."

"Good. Now keep breaking it down. What would we have to do before we win our league?"

"We'd have to have a winning season."

"And before that?"

"We'd have to win one game."

"Right. What would we have to do before we win that first game?"

"We'd have to get a touchdown."

"Yes. And what would we have to do before that?"

"We'd have to get a first down," (advance the ball ten yards in four plays or less).

Then the coach says, "That's right boys. To become a legend, we'll have to get more first downs than any team in history. So focus on getting first downs."

> Therefore, since we are surrounded by such a great cloud of witnesses, let us throw off everything that hinders and the sin that so easily entangles, and let us run with perseverance *the race marked out for us.*
> —HEBREWS 12:1, EMPHASIS ADDED

God wants to help you see the vision of winning the race. He wants you to see yourself holding the trophy. Once God helps you see the vision for your life He will help you *mark out your race.* That's where you will break your big dream into small measurable goals so you can get started. Then, as you cross one marker at a time you will know you are making progress. Knowing you are progressing toward making a dream a reality gives you tremendous courage to keep persevering.

Are you a legend in the making? Personally, I would like to write many books and through them teach millions of people about Christ. That's why when I determine to write a book I write three pages a day. I mark out my race. Life is short. I must keep moving toward my dream. I see the vision. It gives me strength. Just three pages a day and I know I am moving forward. In fact, if I keep it up, I can become a prolific writer.

To have the great enduring perseverance of our Lord, we must not merely see an earthly vision. We must look through our pains and problems to see the person of God and the joys we will experience as we live forever with Him in eternal glory.

"By faith he [Moses] left Egypt, not fearing the king's anger; he persevered because he saw him who is invisible" (Heb. 11:27). Moses persevered because he looked through his present difficulties and saw the person of God.

The apostle Paul's great perseverance was in direct proportion to his ability to see through it to it. "Therefore we do not lose heart. Though outwardly we are wasting away, yet inwardly we are being renewed day by day. For our light and momentary troubles are achieving for us an eternal glory that far outweighs them all. So we fix our eyes not on what is seen, but on what is unseen. For what is seen is temporary, but what is unseen is eternal" (2 Cor. 4:16–18).

Somewhere I heard this poem:

> Two prisoners were looking
> out through the bars.
> One saw mud
> The other saw stars.

What are you looking at? If your focus is on your present difficulties, you are only looking down at the mud. But if you will look up, you will see the reason for which God created you—a dream whereby you can bring Him massive glory.

The apostle Paul had persevered through whippings, beatings, stonings, shipwrecks, slander, hunger, sleepless nights, rejection, betrayals, and misunderstandings. His dream of preaching Christ where Christ was not known, and his vision of winning more souls, helped him get through everything. There was one more big hurdle ahead—his beheading at the hands of the insane Roman Emperor Nero. But Paul's dream burned even brighter as he endured his final days in a miserable prison. He was looking right through his present suffering to the desired fulfillment of his dream—being conformed completely to Christ's image:

> I want to know Christ and the power of his resurrection and the fellowship of sharing in his sufferings, becoming like him in his death, and so, somehow, to attain to the resurrection from the dead. Not that I have already obtained all this, or have already been made perfect, but I press on to take hold of that for which Christ Jesus took hold of me. Brothers, I do not consider myself yet to have taken hold of it. But one thing I do: Forgetting what is behind and straining toward what is ahead, I press on toward the goal to win the prize for which God has called me heavenward in Christ Jesus.
>
> —PHILIPPIANS 3:10–14

Paul was always looking forward to a dream, a vision, a prize, a finish line. As his life neared its earthly conclusion he dreamed of being like Jesus in his death—so full of virtue that he would not be cursing his killers, but forgiving them. Let us not look backward at what we have suffered. Forget about those who have wronged you. *Forgive* and forget. Do not look around at the present problems. Look at the goal line—the prize of being made just like Jesus and the pleasure of bringing Him massive glory. Look through it to it.

Many ministers fall into sexual sin and ruin their lives and ministries. I have never committed adultery, never bought porn, or looked at a pornographic Web site. I pray for wisdom to avoid the trap behind the cheese. I pray for love so that I will always be too tender-hearted to do selfish things and exploit anyone. I pray for purity and self-control. But besides that, I have a special heavenly vision I am heading to. What I am going to helps me get through this world of sin. John wrote:

> Then I looked, and there before me was the Lamb, standing on Mount Zion, and with him 144,000 who had his name and his Father's name written on their foreheads. And I heard a sound from heaven like the roar of rushing waters and like a loud peal of thunder. The sound I heard was like that of harpists playing their harps. And they sang a new song before the throne and before the four living creatures and the elders. No one could learn the song except the 144,000 who had been redeemed from the earth. These are those who did not defile themselves with women, for they kept themselves pure. They follow the Lamb wherever he goes. They were purchased from among men and offered as firstfruits to God and the Lamb. No lie was found in their mouths; they are blameless.
>
> —REVELATION 14:1–5

I always have loved the idea of being one of these people who follow Jesus all over. I would rather follow Him all over heaven than to merely live in a nice mansion and just have Him come and visit me once in a while. Being married is not a defilement because the Bible says the marriage bed is undefiled. (See Heb. 13:4.) So, just in case I could be one of these "first fruit guys," I pass up the opportunities to be immoral.

I would not want to jeopardize my chance of getting to follow Jesus all over heaven. I also avoid immorality because I fear God and do not want to go to hell.

There's a principle in those verses, no matter how you interpret them or who you think that company is. *The principle is that God rewards purity.* If I am not rewarded by getting to be in that company—I will get some other great reward. Daniel and his three friends proved that. When they chose to avoid alcoholic drinks and unclean meats God rewarded them with special spiritual gifts. (See Daniel 1.)

That has worked real well for me. It is a vision of what I am going to and it has helped me get through all kinds of sexual temptations. In Omaha, there was one young woman who hated her husband. She was beautiful and made it clear she wanted a relationship with me. She said to me, "I have always wanted to have a relationship with a man of God." *Yeah—her and her demon*, I thought. She stayed to the end of every service trying to get alone with me. I had other staff members stay with me until I drove away.

When the devil could not use her to destroy my life, he used her to destroy an up-and-coming young minister. This young man, who was preparing for the ministry, started giving her attention. She divorced her husband and abandoned her kids to move in with that young man. Whatever evil was influencing her had made me its first target—but gave up and picked on someone less prepared to handle temptation.

My wife is a very beautiful woman to whom I am highly attracted. We have a wonderful emotional connection as well. I wrote her a song and one of the verses goes, "Some knots come loose so soon after they're tied. Some knots get tighter when the pressure's applied. It is not an accident that we're so tight, because we held on with all our might." We have been through all kinds of things that could have torn us apart. Our marital knot has not come loose—it has gotten tighter.

As much as I love Bonnie, my sexual purity is determined more by my loyalty to Jesus. I would not want to hurt Bonnie or lose her. But even more, I would not want to hurt Jesus or lose out on my opportunity to be intimate with Him. I would not want to miss the reward God gives for purity. I just love the idea of following Jesus all over the place. Friend, that works for me. I am going to it—so I can get through it.

May God give you a vision and a dream to pursue. Even more, may your desire to have eternal intimacy with Christ help you to persevere as Moses did. "He persevered because he saw Him who is invisible" (Heb. 11:27).

> Blessed is the man who perseveres under trial, because when he has stood the test, he will receive the crown of life that God has promised to those who love him.
>
> —JAMES 1:12

Chapter 12
GET IN THE KIND OF TROUBLE GOD LIKES

To the weak I became weak, to win the weak. I have become all things to all men so that by all possible means I might save some.
—1 Corinthians 9:22—

There is a kind of trouble God likes. If you get in the right kind of trouble, God will get in that trouble with you. When God's in the trouble with you, it becomes glorious victory. If we are not having glorious victory it is usually because we're not in enough trouble to attract God's attention.

I learned this principle in the 1970s when I was directing a large bus ministry. From October of 1972 until August 1, 1979, I poured myself into wining children. We would "net" in an area of about five thousand people by having a bus work a pattern through it. A privately owned van equipped with a CB radio would pick up children that lived off the main route. Then the van would intercept the bus several times and load these children onto the bus. Doing this saved thirty minutes per route, allowed us to get twenty to thirty more children per bus, and allowed us to enlist bus riders on any street or alley in a metro area of over one hundred sixty thousand people in

Eugene and Springfield, Oregon.

We called our team of workers "The God Squad." Besides having a CB radio on every bus and privately owned van we had a big "base station" at the church with a huge antenna. That allowed us to communicate with every vehicle while they were on their routes. All this required many workers, hundreds of hours of visitation and a good deal of money. It was a lot of trouble, but we harvested a lot of souls. Thousands of children found Christ as Savior during those years.

> Where there are no oxen, the manger is empty, but from
> the strength of an ox comes an abundant harvest.
>
> —PROVERBS 14:4

I cleaned a lot of mangers when I was growing up on a cattle ranch. The rotten hay in a dirty manger stinks like manure, and every few months, it must be cleaned out. That process is messy. The only way to avoid the mess is to not have cattle in a feedlot. As in the proverb, if you have a bus ministry, you'll have a lot of mess, but also a large harvest of souls.

One of our older buses had a leaky radiator, and I had mechanics take it in for repair. I went out and signed up more kids to ride the buses and when I returned that radiator was sitting in the hallway, all rusty brown with a note in the top. The note said, "Wes, this radiator is shot. It leaks along the bottom. There is a replacement for one hundred dollars, but it is five-and-a-half inches taller. Call if you have any questions. Jim."

I knew if I asked the pastor for one hundred dollars, he would say we were broke. We had exhausted our resources bringing in these children. We had built bleachers up the walls in the classrooms. We had an usher stand in the boys bathroom to make sure five little boys used the toilet before flushing it. The reason—so many kids were flushing the toilets we were blowing the lids off the septic tanks. The pastor had great administrative ability and we were juggling kids from our church to a local school gym. While half were in Sunday school the other half had children's church in that gym.

As I walked toward the office, I knew bus three had to run. My friend Pat Burgess was the bus captain. At least fifty kids would be on his bus. Out of the fifty kids, at least five would be brand new. Those five would receive the Lord when our children's pastors, Gene and Starlene McDaniels, presented the gospel to them. That bus just had to run. That's all I knew.

When I entered the church office, Mae Ricks, the secretary, exploded in joy, "There's been a miracle. Jesus appeared to a man and told him to give you one hundred dollars." I took that check and headed to the auto repair shop. The replacement radiator was brand new, but an odd size. They had discounted it from something like two hundred dollars down to just one hundred. I bought it and told the volunteer mechanics to put it in Bus three."

Those men had to cut off a little bit of the bracing under the hood which allowed it to barely clip down over that extra tall radiator. We ran the bus on Sunday. Two weeks later, the man who had the vision of Jesus asked to take me to lunch. He told me this story in person. He was fixing a fire in a wood stove in his warehouse when he heard a voice say, "Kneel and pray." As he knelt he saw a white robe. He looked up the robe into the face of Jesus Christ. Jesus stretched out His hand and said, *I want you to take that one hundred dollars you received in the mail today and give it to Wes. He's in trouble with his buses.*

The man began to cry, overwhelmed at the Lord's presence, "But Lord, I do not know anybody named Wes."

Jesus said, *Wes at Goshen.* The man cried all the more and said, "But Lord, I do not know any Wes at Goshen." Jesus told him, *Call Bob Tennant at Willamette Greystone. He'll know what to do.* Then Jesus disappeared.

Bob Tennant was one of our church ushers. He sold bricks and this man was a brick mason, so they knew each other through the business connection. The man was overwrought with emotion when he called Bob and said, "Bob, get over here quick."

Brother Tennant thought perhaps the man's wife had died or something. When he got there, the two of them wept and had a prayer meeting—until they remembered why Jesus appeared. Then they got in a car and drove the check to Goshen. They had just left it when I returned to find the note in the old radiator.

That was nearly thirty years ago. All through my ministry I have remembered that Jesus did not appear over the Senate, White House, or the Supreme Court. He appeared over a radiator for an old bus that brought little kids to church. *He was with me when I was in trouble winning souls.*

> He will call upon me, and I will answer him; I will be with him in trouble, I will deliver him and honor him.
>
> —PSALM 91:15

There's plenty of trouble to go through in the ministry. Jesus did not say, *Wes is in trouble in the ministry.* He basically said, *Wes is in trouble winning souls—he's in trouble with his buses.* When pastors and churches feel like the Lord is nowhere to be found, they need to get in more trouble than they are already in. The trouble with most churches is that they are not in enough trouble winning souls. Winning souls to Christ attracts the attention of God like nothing else.

I wish everyone could have met Dr. Bernard Johnson. It is estimated that three million people came to Christ in his stadium crusades. I wish there were books about the great exploits God used him to do in Brazil. It was my privilege to meet him at a Light For The Lost rally in Springfield, Missouri.

During one banquet where he was speaking a tornado passed directly over our hotel complex. We evacuated to the halls of the hotel and sat down with pillows over our heads. While others prayed for their lives I took the opportunity to sit down next to Dr. Johnson and show him my soul-winning booklet *How to Receive the Life of God*. I wanted him to put it into Portuguese.

We survived the tornado and several weeks later he called me to say he liked the booklet and would put it into Portuguese if I could raise five thousand dollars. I prayed and God told me to call David Burdine. Mr. Burdine heads the Bethesda Foundation. I said, "God told me you'd give five thousand dollars to put my book in Portuguese for Dr. Bernard Johnson." He said, "I do not know you, but I know Bernard Johnson and if he wants your book I will be happy to give his ministry the five thousand dollars." Twenty thousand booklets were printed and used in Brazil.

That's how I came to know this mighty man of God. Eventually I talked him into coming to speak at my church in Omaha, Nebraska. He told this story to our church.

On the day that Mozambique was taken over by communists Brother Johnson landed in the capital. He was immediately arrested and charged with being an agent for the Central Intelligence Agency (CIA). They took him into a room were a captain and nine other men surrounded him. They were going to torture him until he confessed to what they were charging him with.

The captain tried to hit him in the face but an invisible supernatural shield stopped the man's fist about three inches from Bernard's face. Over and over, with all his might, this torture captain tried to mar the face of the great soul winner.

After a half hour of this, Bernard became so emboldened that he stood up and said, "You've had your turn, now it is my turn." He closed the door and stood against it. He said, "I am going to tell you men the gospel and none of you are getting out of here until I am finished." He preached to them for twenty minutes and then opened the door and said, "Now you may go." They all rushed out of the room, leaving him alone.

As soon as they left the room God opened his eyes and he saw thousands of angels forming a column above his head. The angels had drawn swords and God said to him, "I did not let that little man touch you. If he had, these angels would have killed him immediately."

Just then the little torture captain returned and said, "I have just called the head of our revolution. He say's he'll give you fifty thousand dollars U.S. if you can tell him how to get a force field of protection like the one you have." Dr. Johnson then told him about the angels and why God had shielded him—to prevent the angels from killing that captain. At that, in terror, the captain ushered Bernard out into the street and released him.

Very few men have stayed in as much continual trouble winning souls as Dr. Bernard Johnson. Jesus was with him in trouble, giving him strength to persevere.

I tell Dr. Johnson's story and my miracle radiator story to inspire you so that you will soon experience your own unique fulfillment of Christ's promise. He said that if we'd go forth making disciples, He would be with us to the very end of the age. (See Matthew 28:19–20.) He'll keep that promise in some special way that will demonstrate He is with you in trouble—as long as you are in trouble winning souls.

If your troubles seem overwhelming to you—get in more trouble than you are already in. This is an elementary, and very logical course of action if you have a faith mentality. *Why wallow around in boring trouble when you could add some really exciting trouble to the mix?* If you will get in trouble winning souls, your situation will become irresistible to God. He cannot stay out of a really good soul-winning rumble. He'll roll up His sleeves and jump into your situation with His holy zeal.

Even when I do not see Jesus, I know Him well enough to be assured that as long as I am winning souls He is with me. This gives me strength to persevere. Knowing I am in the right kind of trouble is a comfort to my heart and mind. The knowledge that Jesus is with me in my troubles helps me persevere. I intend to stay in the right kind of trouble all my life.

> Do not merely listen to the word, and so deceive your-selves. Do what it says.
>
> —JAMES 1:22

What's your plan to get in trouble? There's something you could be doing right now to help win souls. Find out what that is and do it with all your might. Then, purpose to stay in trouble winning souls the rest of your life.

CONCLUSION

The appendix of this book lists these twelve principles of perseverance. Whether you are a spiritual leader or a layman, you will need to put these into practice to fulfill whatever ministry God has called you to. More than that, these principles will help you do the will of God in your family, your career, and all your interactions with people.

Whatever great difficulty you are in right now, one or more of these principles, if put into practice, will bring you to victory and great achievement. Then, give all the glory to God and start a new cycle of success. As you depend upon the Lord, He will strengthen you so that you can persevere in obedience, unto victory, and greater intimacy with Jesus.

It is my prayer that these principles will become like dear friends to you—and that you will apply them constantly. *Photocopy this list and keep it handy. Memorize it.* May your life bring massive glory to the Lord Jesus Christ as you keep on obeying Him in persevering love. May you be among those who receive the promise of Jesus in John 14:21–23. May Jesus reveal Himself to you and through you. May you cross the finish line as a true spiritual champion and receive the rewards of the overcomers.

I love you. God bless you.

AFTERWORD

This is the Cycle of Success: depend on God, seek God, hear God, obey God, persist in obedience, achieve victory through God, and return the glory to God. Then, go back to dependence and begin a new cycle. Dependence is the top of the cycle. Perseverance is the bottom, and leads to achievement and victory. Perseverance is love that keeps on obeying.

1. Adopt the heart motive of Jesus: John 17:1–5.

2. Pray through—until you hear God or God hears you: Luke 18:1.

3. Examine your thoughts and get God's thoughts: 2 Cor. 10:5.

4. Resist Satan's evaluations and viewpoints: 1 Pet. 5:8–9.

5. Make a deeper commitment to God: Matt. 26:42; Esther 4:11, 16.

6. Celebrate trouble: James 1:2; 2 Cor. 12:9–10.

7. Overcome evil with good. Be generous even in your need: Rom. 12:19–21; Ps. 112:5.

8. Armor up. Meditate on God's Word, (helmet of Salvation). Turn at the correction of the Word, (belt of truth). Practice doing God's Word, (breastplate of righteousness). Memorize God's Word, (boots of readiness). Believe God's Word, (shield of faith). Speak

God's Word, (Sword of the Spirit). Pray in the Spirit daily. Be best friends with the Word of God and the Holy Spirit.

9. Change the equation of weariness on a daily basis. That equation is, "All I know to do + my best effort + a long time = not enough." Inject more knowledge, network, and pray, adding more power, and give all-out commitment in the time factor.

10. Encourage someone else: Prov. 11:25.

11. Have a dream, a vision and break it down into small measurable steps: Heb. 12:1–3.

12. Get in and stay in the kind of trouble God likes best—soul-winning: Matt. 28:18–20; Ps. 91:15.

About the Author

Wes Daughenbaugh is a veteran soul-winner with thirty-four years of experience in full-time ministry, including seven as an associate pastor, eighteen as a senior pastor, and nine as a teacher/evangelist. He is an anointed communicator known for transparency, a "sweet spirit," and an ability to make profound truths simple to understand. His goal is to be a master of encouragement, especially to spiritual leaders. A tangible anointing of holy fire flows through his hands as God wills, and has resulted in many hundreds being baptized in the Holy Spirit, physically healed, or delivered from spiritual oppression.

He is a graduate of Eugene Bible College and is ordained with the Assemblies of God. Wes and his wife, Bonnie, have two daughters and two grandsons.

CONTACT THE AUTHOR

Wes Daughenbaugh
Gospel Net Ministries
PO Box 485
Creswell, OR 97426
Phone: (541) 895-9770
E-mail: wes@gospelnetministries.org
Web site: www.gospelnetministries.org

If you have enjoyed this book, perhaps you would like additional sermons by Wes Daughenbaugh. You can view the teaching series available through his ministry by going to the Web site above.

Wes comes in person to as many churches as possible each year doing Sunday morning services, revivals, and seminars. The emphasis of his ministry is about becoming a Christlike Christian. Each request will be prayerfully considered.

You can subscribe to Wes's monthly spiritual growth club called Partners in Courage. Each month, Wes sends out one new message. It comes with eight pages of detailed outlined notes and a newsletter. Gospel Net Ministries does not use the newsletter to recruit extra funds. You can have the audio message on either CD or cassette tape. The monthly cost for a CD is ten dollars and nine dollars for a cassette tape. Call, write, or e-mail to sign up. When the first message comes, a pre-stamped envelope will be enclosed in which you can send back your payment.